INTERNATIONAL TRADE

INTERNATIONAL TRADE
Theory and
Empirical Evidence

H. ROBERT HELLER
University of California at Los Angeles

Prentice-Hall, Inc., Englewood Cliffs, New Jersey

382
H477

PRENTICE-HALL INTERNATIONAL, INC., *London*
PRENTICE-HALL OF AUSTRALIA, PTY. LTD., *Sydney*
PRENTICE-HALL OF CANADA, LTD., *Toronto*
PRENTICE-HALL OF INDIA PRIVATE LTD., *New Delhi*
PRENTICE-HALL OF JAPAN, INC., *Tokyo*

To **OMA**

Preface

My purpose in writing this book is to assemble the minimum framework required for an understanding of international trade problems. International trade is defined narrowly as the set of problems which arises from and in connection with the exchange of physical commodities between nations. International monetary and financial problems are not treated in this volume. Several books are available to supplement this volume if the whole field of international economics is to be covered.

The approach is geometric throughout. No use of mathematics is required. More than in most other fields of economics has the graphical approach been utilized in international trade. The book tries to put many of the different concepts, which are scattered throughout the literature, into one concise framework. In a sense the book constitutes a tool-kit for the student of international trade without which he might find it difficult to comprehend much of the literature. All unnecessary detail is left aside and attention is concentrated on the systematic development of the analytical framework.

The book is intended for use in a one-quarter or one-semester upper division course in international trade. The level of difficulty is above the introductory textbooks by Ellsworth, Kindleberger, and Snider; and below the advanced graduate treatises by Caves, Kemp, and Vanek, which require prior familiarity with the literature or the use of mathematical techniques that are too sophisticated for the typical undergraduate student. Graduate students might find the present book useful in that it gives them a brief review and a starting point for the study of more advanced topics.

Thanks are due to Professors Richard G. Lipsey and Tibor Scitovsky who first taught me international trade and whose approach to problems of international trade is reflected to a considerable extent in the following pages. Professors Duncan Mac Rae and Peter Clark were kind enough to read the manuscript and to offer many helpful suggestions. Miss Ruth Ann Quick edited and efficiently typed several drafts. More than mere thanks are due to Miss Birgitta Hultgren who rewrote almost the entire manuscript and to Professor William Allen who made a grand total of 156 suggestions which improved the book immensely. I alone am responsible for any remaining imperfections.

H. R. H.

Contents

LIST OF SYMBOLS USED

C   Consumption
CIC   Community Indifference Curve
D   Domestic
EX   Exports
I   Indifference Curve or Isoquant
IM   Imports
K   Capital
L   Labor
O   Origin
OC   Offer Curve
P   Production
TI   Trade Indifference Curve
TOC   Trade Offer Curve
TOT   Terms of Trade

Superscripts

A   Person A
B   Person B
F   France
G   Global
N   Netherlands
U   Union
UK   United Kingdom
US   United States

Subscripts

C   Cloth
i   Any Real Number
T   Tariff
W   Wheat

CHAPTER 1

Theory and Methodology of International Trade

In this introductory chapter we will explore some of the problems of methodology which arise in conjunction with the study of causes and effects of international trade. To do this we must first of all familiarize ourselves with the type of approach or methodology used in attacking specific problems in subsequent chapters. We will also show in this chapter the relationship of these problems to those of general economic theory. The final section will be concerned with problems encountered in connection with empirical verification.

1. Methodology of Economics

Economists are concerned with the problems arising from and in connection with the economic interactions of different economic units. Among all the different problems, we can distinguish two broad groupings: problems of positive economics and problems of normative economics.

a. Positive Economics

Positive economics is concerned with what is. It is concerned with the way the economic system functions and the effects of changes in some variables on other magnitudes. Essentially three steps are involved in constructing a useful economic theory: (1) development of a framework for analysis, (2) construction of various hypotheses, and (3) empirical verification.

(i) The Framework for Analysis

The analytical framework consists basically of a set of concepts to help us state precisely and unambiguously what we shall infer, deduce, predict, or observe. The usefulness of the framework adopted can be judged by the efficiency with which it fulfills this objective.

While the framework has to be specific, it must also provide latitude for expansion and development of the system if this should become necessary. The more operational the definitions are—that is, the better they are adapted to the purpose of the analysis—the easier will be the task of analysis itself.

(ii) Construction of Hypotheses

The second task is to make some analytically useful abstractions from reality. The world as we observe it is much too complex to allow us to draw directly meaningful conclusions about causal relationships. There are many phenomena which have little or no bearing on the issue at hand. The purpose of constructing hypotheses is to achieve order among the multitude of observable phenomena and to eliminate less important factors while focusing attention on important causal links. This is done through a process of abstraction and the formulation of hypotheses about the workings of the economic system.

The set of concepts and hypotheses is often referred to as an economic model. There are two ways in which economic models can be employed usefully: in analysis and in forecasting.

Analytically, the model helps us to check the consistency of the various assumptions made. The effects of changes in the definitions and assumptions can be studied in detail, enabling us to isolate a few key variables which are crucial as far as the logical structure of the model is concerned. These key variables may then be studied more intensively. In this way we will increase our knowledge of the functioning of the economic system studied. To the extent that new insights are revealed by this process, we may want to reformulate our initial model in the light of the experiences gained.

The second function of an economic model is to allow us to make forecasts of probable effects of changes in some variables. In trying to assess the effects of contemplated policy changes, the predictive power of the model should prove most valuable.

(iii) Empirical Verification

Finally, the validity of the predictions which follow from a particular economic model must be subjected to empirical testing. It is possible to construct an infinite number of logically consistent models which may yield conflicting results. Only the empirical verification of the different economic predictions which the alternative models may yield will allow us to decide which model is the most accurate and useful one. The ultimate goal is to gain more insight into the functioning of the economic system, and empirical testing helps us to separate the useful economic models from the irrelevant ones.

b. Normative Economics

In contrast to positive economics, concerned with what is, normative economics is concerned with what ought to be. Normative economics, by definition, requires value judgments. Normative economics is involved both with the selection of rules to judge welfare changes and with the evaluation of the welfare changes themselves. Once a yardstick with which to assess the economic consequences of different economic policies is found, the task of determining the most desirable or beneficial course of action is made considerably easier. Often we will not be in a position to devise a yardstick which will be acceptable to everyone concerned. Under these conditions the application of different value systems may yield different results about the desirability of certain economic actions. Unfortunately, these differences cannot be settled by resorting to empirical testing procedures, since a value system which is logically consistent cannot be found superior or inferior to other logically consistent value systems by empirical methods.

2. Reasons for a Special Theory of International Trade

International trade theory can be regarded as an extension of general economic theory to the special problems encountered in trade between nations. While the emphasis has traditionally been on trade between countries, the theory can also be applied to problems of trade between other economic units: trade between individuals like Robinson Crusoe and Friday poses theoretical problems similar to those between cities during the Middle Ages or in the time of the Hanseatic League. Today we may be interested in trade between different economic regions within one country; for example, between California and the rest of the United States. Much of international trade theory will find a fruitful application here. While trade theory can be applied to all the problem areas mentioned, there are still several reasons to continue referring to the theory as international trade theory rather than as general trade theory.

First of all, there are several *economic* reasons for concentrating our attention on nations as the basic economic units. As a general rule, there is a vast difference in the degree of mobility of resources between countries as opposed to within countries. Human beings, the factor of production labor, are often restricted in their freedom of movement between countries, while they are free to select their residence within countries. Immigration laws,

different licensing requirements for professional people, citizenship requirements for government employees, and other obstacles inhibit the free flow of
labor between countries. Similarly, financial transactions within countries are
usually unrestrained, while international capital flows are often prohibited
or severely limited by governmental authorities.

Another important resource, land, is virtually immobile internationally.
Short of declaring war and conquering territory, it is difficult to conceive
how nations could transfer land among themselves. The time when it was not
unusual to purchase territories from other nations seems to have passed
forever.

Also, we will find that economic units located within the same country
are subject to the same rates of taxation, have to raise funds in the same
capital markets, and must use much of the same economic infrastructure,
such as communication, transportation, and information facilities. Thus the
whole economic environment of individual economic units is much more
homogeneous within a country than it is between economic units located
in different countries.

Secondly, the *sociopolitical* environment differs greatly between nations,
while it is more uniform within countries. Households and business firms in
the same country operate within the same legal framework, are subject to the
same social institutions, and are ruled by the same government. Similar habits
and business customs prevail within the national boundaries, making it easier
for businessmen to deal with other economic units even if geographically far
removed. All these conditions hold only rarely, and then imperfectly, with
reference to trade between different nations. Often it is much easier and more
convenient for a San Diego firm to arrange a business deal with a New York
firm than to turn to a geographically much nearer firm in Tijuana, Mexico.

There is a third, and much less important, reason for looking at international trade problems apart from other economic problems: there has been
for a considerable time a rather strong *specialization of some economists* in the
international trade field. As a result, we find that international trade theory
has developed its own body of literature, often employing methods which
differ slightly from those used in other branches of economics. For instance,
a relatively large amount of international trade theory relies to a great extent
on general equilibrium analysis, and does not restrict itself to the problems of
partial equilibrium which characterize much of traditional price theory. Most
of international trade theory deals with several commodities, several factors
of production, and several countries simultaneously. The greater complexity
of the analysis has led to the development of special techniques for dealing
with these problems. One consequence of this specialization within economics
is that international trade theory has tended to either antedate or lag behind
the developments in general economic theory. International trade specialists,
for example, held to the labor theory of value for a much longer time than

did economists in most other fields. On the other hand, much of modern welfare economics was first elaborated within the framework of international trade theory.

3. Assumptions of the Theory of International Trade

International trade theory has to deal with a greater number of variables at any given time than do most other fields of economics. In order to keep the theories manageable and compact, certain assumptions are usually made in the first stage of the analysis. All these assumptions can be removed, one by one, but only at the cost of increasing the complexity of the models. At this point it may be useful to make explicit the more important assumptions which we will make in the beginning of our analysis. Several of these assumptions will be dropped as we progress to more complicated and comprehensive models of trade, but others will be maintained throughout the volume.

The first of the major simplifying assumptions is that all of the real variables of the economic system are determined independently of the monetary system. This assumption is often referred to as the *neutrality of money*. In such a case all real and monetary variables are determined completely independently of each other. The real sector is concerned with questions of *relative prices*, e.g., how many packages of cigarettes can be exchanged for one loaf of bread, or how many hours of work will earn one pizza. All that concerns us are rates of exchange between different commodities or factors of production (or their respective services). We deal with a pure barter economy in which monetary magnitudes have no influence on relative prices. The only function that money performs is to set the *absolute* price level. It is easy to see that in this system it is immaterial whether all monetary magnitudes within the economy are doubled, tripled, or halved; relative prices will not be influenced, and nobody will be either better or worse off. At times some countries have changed their monetary unit with precisely this result. France did so in 1960, when one hundred old francs were declared to be the same as one new franc. All prices were reduced to one hundredth of their previous level; so were all wages, assets, and liabilities. Nothing really changed except that the decimal place in all financial statements was moved two digits to the left. As a matter of fact, the old franc notes continued to circulate along with the new ones for a long period of time.

A second important assumption is that *all prices are truly flexible*, and that they are determined under conditions of perfect competition. In other words, there are no economic, political, or other considerations which impede the free interplay of the forces of supply and demand in the determination of prices for any items. Thus we postulate the absence of minimum wage laws, maximum rents, fixed prices for certain commodities, and other restraints to price flexibility, as well as the nonexistence of monopolistic imperfections.

On the production side we will assume initially that the total *amount of factors of production is fixed* for any one country. Thus we will ignore the effects that changes in factor prices might have on the quantities which are effectively available. Increases in the wage rate, therefore, will not lead to increases in the labor force participation rate or in the number of hours worked. Higher land rents will not lead to irrigation and reclamation of previously unused land. And the total amount of capital resources of the economy is assumed to be fixed. This assumption implies that the supply curves for all factors of production are vertical straight lines; i.e., that they are completely inelastic.

Closely associated with the assumption of fixed domestic factor supplies is the assumption of *international immobility of factors*. While factors are assumed to be completely mobile within countries, moving in response to the highest reward offered, we postulate that they are completely immobile between countries. The arguments in favor of this assumption have already been presented and need not be repeated here.

We will assume also that the *technology* available to and used by all producers of the same product within one country is the same. The production functions within one country are therefore identical. No patents or privileged information will restrict the use of any techniques of production to a group of business firms. On the other hand, production functions may well be different in various countries.

On the demand side of our analysis, *tastes* are assumed to be given. In other words, the indifference maps showing the preference patterns of the consumers are given and invariant, so that no changes in taste will occur as a result of the sudden availability of certain internationally traded goods.

In the same vein, we assume that *income distribution* patterns are given and known. A shift in income distribution patterns in conjunction with dissimilar taste patterns of the different economic groups affected by the change in income distribution can give rise to many problems relevant to international trade.

As does most of the international trade literature, we will assume throughout that there are no barriers to trade in the form of costs of *transportation, information*, and *communication*. All these costs would impose additional burdens on the traders, which would in most cases lead to a reduction in the volume of international trade. As a matter of fact, any one of these costs may be so great that trade would cease completely.

Finally, it should be noted that, owing to our assumptions of flexible prices and neutrality of money, the full utilization of all productive resources within the economy is always assured. All factors of production available at the current prices and wage rates will be employed in the productive process.

Prices and wages will adjust to equate the quantities supplied and demanded in different markets. Excess supplies or shortages of commodities do not occur.

4. Basic Considerations of International Trade Theory

The pure theory of international trade involves four basic considerations. (1) What determines the *direction of trade?* Here we are interested in why a country tends to export one commodity rather than another. (2) Intimately connected with the direction of trade is the question of the physical *volume* of international trade and the *prices* at which the commodities are traded. Clearly, countries will not only be interested in knowing whether they should be exporting bananas or radios, but they will also want to know in what quantity these commodities can be exported and what prices their products will command in the world markets. (3) The effects of *trade restrictions* are also of interest. The imposition of tariffs and other restrictive devices will change many of the crucial variables, as will the formation of customs unions or common markets. Finally, (4) we will be concerned with the effect of free trade and restricted trade on the *economic welfare* of the countries under consideration. This is doubtlessly significant, since one of the most important economic goals is to make all persons as well off as they can possibly be without making anyone else worse off. The first three problem areas mentioned are problems of positive economics, while the fourth problem belongs in the sphere of normative economics.

Note on Procedure

In the following pages we will utilize the sequence of analysis presented in Section 1-1 as closely as is practicable. The model developed in this book is built up step by step in the early chapters and is put "through the paces" in the last few chapters. The reader unfamiliar with intermediate price theory is well advised to first study the Appendix, where many of the concepts used in the book are introduced and explained. Chapter 1 gives a brief introduction to the problem area treated in this book and the methodology used. The next four chapters deal with the reasons for the emergence of international trade. The emphasis in Chapter 2 is on differences in technology. In Chapter 3 it is on differences in factor endowments, and in Chapter 4 it is on tastes. Chapter 5 shows the interaction of these three factors in determining the direction and structure of international trade. The following two chapters concentrate attention on the factors of production: Chapter 6 is concerned with the effects of international trade on the factors of production, and Chapter 7 with the effects of changes in the factors of production, especially those due to economic growth, on international trade. Normative aspects dominate in Chapter 8, which deals with the effects of international trade on economic welfare. The theory of restricted trade is outlined in the last two chapters: the theory of general trade restrictions via tariffs is the topic of Chapter 9, while Chapter 10 concentrates on selective trade restrictions via customs unions. Empirical evidence relevant to the topic discussed is presented at the end of each chapter.

SUGGESTED FURTHER READINGS

Baumol, William J., *Business Behavior, Value and Growth* (2nd ed.). New York: Harcourt, Brace, and World, 1967, Chapter 1.

Caves, Richard, *Trade and Economic Structure*. Cambridge: Harvard University Press, 1960, Chapter 1.

Friedman, Milton, "The Methodology of Positive Economics," in *Essays in Positive Economics*. Chicago: University of Chicago Press, 1953.

Haberler, Gottfried, *The Theory of International Trade*. London: Hodge, 1936, Introduction, Chapter 9.

Vanek, Jaroslav, *International Trade: Theory and Economic Policy*. Homewood, Ill.: Richard D. Irwin, 1962, Chapters 1, 11.

CHAPTER 2

The Theory
of Comparative Costs

1. The Real Cost Theory

International trade theory as a special field of economic inquiry was first systematically developed by a group of economists now referred to as the "classical" economists. Although no one of these economists is likely to have held all the views later attributed to this school, Adam Smith, David Ricardo, John Stuart Mill, and Frank Taussig can nevertheless be considered as exponents of the classical doctrine. The international trade theory which they developed not only constitutes the beginning of international trade theory as such, but also serves as a simple starting point for our inquiry into the causes and effects of international trade. Only after we have mastered their simple model will it be possible to tackle the more complex and, it is hoped, more realistic models.

a. Direction of Trade

The classical economists focused their attention primarily on the *gains from trade* in order to show that free international trade would benefit the trading countries. Implicit in their writings is also a theory of the *structure of trade*. Here the determinants of the direction of trade will occupy our attention first.

We can observe specialization in production, or division of labor, on different levels of the economic system: individual persons specialize in different occupations, firms specialize in certain products. The same is true for economic regions and for countries. The specialized economic units may then want to exchange or trade some of their products.

Ricardo is generally credited with having been the first economist to recognize the importance of differences in *relative* or, as he called it, *com-*

parative costs as the basis for international trade. His model of international trade contains several simplifying assumptions. In addition to the assumptions already mentioned in Chapter 1, Ricardo assumes the validity of the *labor theory of value*, which holds that there is one productive factor of importance as far as the value of a commodity is concerned: labor. Commodities which require different amounts of labor for their production will have different values, where the value of the commodity is directly proportional to the amount of labor required for its production. The output per unit of labor input is assumed to be constant over all relevant ranges of the production function.

Other factors of production, such as land and capital equipment, are assumed to be either (1) of no significance, (2) so evenly spread over all labor inputs that they always work in a fixed proportion with labor, or (3) merely representing stored-up labor. This latter assumption is particularly relevant to capital goods, because labor has originally been used in the production of these goods, and thus determines their value.

More sophisticated versions of the labor theory of value recognize the notion of different levels of irksomeness or disutility associated with the performance of different types of labor. In this case all labor units must first be transformed into standard units—simple unskilled labor, for example—and then the value of the commodities produced will again conform to the amount of standardized labor units embodied in them.

It may be helpful at this juncture to introduce a simple numerical example of Ricardo's theory of comparative costs. Let us assume that there are two countries in this world, the United Kingdom and the United States, and that they produce only two commodities, cloth and wheat. If both countries use all the factors of production available to them, each might be able to produce either the quantity of cloth or the quantity of wheat (expressed in some appropriate unit) shown in Table 2-1.

TABLE 2-1

| | Possible Physical Output of | |
	Cloth	or	Wheat
United Kingdom	100	50
United States	200	150

The data in Table 2-1 show the *production possibility schedule* of the two countries. The same information is shown graphically in the *production possibility curves* of Figures 2-1 and 2-2.

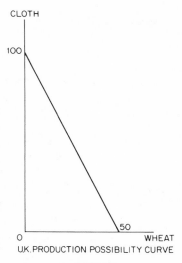

FIGURE 2-1

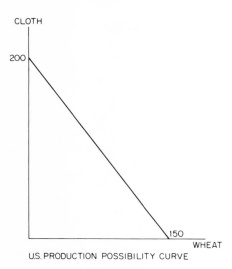

FIGURE 2-2

If the two countries do *not* trade with each other, we will find that cloth and wheat exchange in the two countries in the following ratios:

U. K.   1 Cloth = .50 Wheat
U. S.   1 Cloth = .75 Wheat

The physical exchange ratios that will be established accurately reflect the relative amounts of labor used up in the production of cloth and wheat in the two countries. British workers are able to produce exactly twice as much cloth as wheat; thus each unit of wheat actually produced embodies twice the amount of labor embodied in a unit of cloth, and each unit of wheat will therefore be twice as valuable as a unit of cloth.

We note that the United Kingdom can produce absolutely less of both commodities than the United States. Yet the United Kingdom has a *comparative* advantage in the production of cloth. For each additional unit of cloth produced, the United Kingdom has to give up only .50 units of wheat, while the United States has to give up .75 units. Relatively speaking, the amount of wheat which the United Kingdom has to give up for each additional unit of cloth is less than it is for the United States, resulting in a steeper production possibility curve for the United Kingdom than for the United States.

If we introduce now the possibility of international trade between the United Kingdom and the United States, the British will soon realize that they can exchange one unit of cloth in the United States for .75 units of wheat, while they will be able to obtain only .50 units of wheat in the domestic market for the same unit of cloth. The British cloth manufacturer who obtains his wheat in the United States rather than at home is therefore able to obtain .25 units of wheat more per unit of cloth exchanged. As a consequence, it will be to Britain's advantage to import wheat from the United States in exchange for cloth.

The reverse argument applies to the United States, where wheat farmers can exchange one unit of wheat against one and a third units of cloth, while they could obtain two units of cloth in Britain. Naturally, they will tend to import their cloth from the United Kingdom in exchange for wheat.

The result of our analysis so far is that the United Kingdom will tend to export cloth and import wheat, while the United States will tend to export wheat and import cloth. The *direction* of international trade is in this way determined. We can restate our findings as follows:

A country will tend to export the commodity whose relative (to the other commodity) cost or comparative cost of production is lower than it is in the other country.

Note, too, that if there are no differences in relative costs of production, i.e., a situation of identical comparative costs, then there will be no incentive for trade. Graphically, this is expressed by parallel production possibility curves.

No international trade will occur if there are no differences in relative production costs between countries.

b. Limits of the International Terms of Trade

After having solved the problem of the direction of international trade, we will direct our attention to the problem of the determination of the physical exchange ratio and the relative prices of the commodities traded. We will restrict our analysis at this point to the determinants of the upper and lower limits of these ratios. A full analysis of the precise determination will be postponed until we have incorporated demand patterns into our analysis. However, cost considerations alone will allow us to make some inferences about the magnitude of the international exchange ratios.

Before free trade starts, we have one distinct domestic exchange ratio of cloth against wheat for each of the two countries. After the opening up of trade relations, these two different exchange ratios will be replaced by a single exchange ratio, namely, the world market exchange ratio. This world market exchange ratio is generally referred to as the *terms of trade*.

We note now that the United Kingdom will not be interested in exporting cloth if it does not bring *at least* .50 units of wheat for each unit of cloth. This is the domestic pretrade exchange ratio, and any smaller quantity of wheat offered by the United States will be refused because British farmers themselves are able to produce .50 units of wheat with the same amount of resources as required for one unit of cloth production. At any exchange ratio which is better than .50 units of wheat for a unit of cloth, British producers will be only too happy to export cloth. In the previous section we found that the United Kingdom will tend to export cloth in exchange for wheat, and now we have some additional information on the *minimum* exchange ratio of wheat for cloth at which this exchange will take place.

On the other hand, United States farmers will not be willing to trade internationally if they have to give up more than .75 units of wheat for each unit of cloth, that is, more than the amount which they would have to pay in the domestic market. This will set a *maximum* for the wheat/cloth exchange ratio, since it gives the maximum quantity of wheat which they are willing to exchange against a unit of cloth.

In this way we have determined the lower and upper limits of the wheat/cloth exchange ratio. If the world terms of trade should for any reason fall outside these limits, *both* countries will want to export the same commodity and import the other commodity—a situation which cannot be realized in our two-country world. If, let us say, the exchange ratio were initially established at one cloth for one wheat unit, both countries would want to import wheat because they would get more wheat than they themselves could conceivably produce if they were to cut back their cloth production by one unit and devote these resources to wheat production. Yet, as there is no country willing to export wheat in a one-to-one ratio for cloth, their import desires will be frustrated.

The international exchange ratio of the commodities traded will have to lie between the limits established by the pretrade domestic exchange ratios.

c. Equilibrium Conditions for the International Terms of Trade

After having determined the upper and lower bounds of the region into which the international terms of trade must fall, we are left with the question of the precise determination of the terms of trade. Like any other competitive exchange ratio, the international terms of trade are determined by supply and demand for the products in world markets. Up to this point we have discussed only the influence of production, or supply conditions, on international trade and exchange ratios. The role of demand patterns in this context is considered in Chapter 4, and consequently the answer to the question of the precise determination of the international terms of trade will have to be postponed until Chapter 5, when all our tools of analysis are assembled.

There is, however, no reason why we cannot discuss the *equilibrium conditions* which will have to be fulfilled if the international terms of trade are to be stable. With any given set of terms of trade, the United States will be willing to export a certain quantity of one commodity in exchange for a given quantity of the other commodity. The same will hold true for the United Kingdom. It is evident that the markets will be cleared only if the quantities that one country wishes to export and the quantities that the other country wishes to import are identical for every commodity. Only then will there be no further tendency for the international terms of trade to change. We can state this condition formally:

$$IM_i^{US} = EX_i^{UK} \quad \text{(where } i \text{ stands for a particular commodity)} \quad (2\text{-}1)$$

and

$$EX_i^{US} = IM_i^{UK} \tag{2-2}$$

If this condition is not fulfilled, then the quantities that countries want to export and import do not exactly match, and there will be either surpluses or deficits in the international markets. If there is an excess supply of a commodity in the world markets, then exporters will eventually be willing to offer a larger quantity of this commodity in exchange for other commodities. Thus the terms of trade will adjust themselves until the quantities supplied and demanded match exactly. This is the equilibrium condition for the terms of trade. To repeat: while we do not yet know *how* the equilibrium exchange ratio is determined in world markets, we are able to state the conditions that have to be satisfied if the exchange ratio is to be in equilibrium.

The international commodity exchange ratios (terms of trade) will be in equilibrium if the quantities of all commodities that countries wish to export are equal to the quantities of all commodities that countries wish to import at these exchange ratios.

2. The Opportunity Cost Theory

In the previous section we examined the classical theory of the structure of trade, as formulated by Ricardo and refined by Taussig and others. One of the fundamental premises of this theory is the labor theory of value. This restrictive assumption of the classical theory can be discarded in favor of a more general framework without otherwise changing the basic argument. This more modern approach was first formulated by Gottfried Haberler[1] and is customarily referred to as the *opportunity cost theory* of international trade. His basic contention is that the relative prices of different commodities are determined by cost differentials, where costs do not refer to the amounts of labor required to produce a commodity, but to the alternative production which has to be foregone to allow for the production of the commodity in question. In case several alternatives have to be foregone, the highest valued alternative determines the opportunity cost of the commodity in question. The value of each commodity can therefore be reckoned in terms of opportunity costs reflecting foregone production of other commodities.

---

[1] Gottfried Haberler, *The Theory of International Trade* (London: Hodge, 1936).

This formulation means that the quantities of resources employed in the production of a commodity do not enter into consideration at all, because attention is focused solely on the choice between final products. We are not concerned with how many factors or how much of each factor is required to produce a commodity, but rather with the other products which could have been produced with these factors.

The opportunity cost theory represents an improvement over the real cost theory in two respects: (1) by dropping the assumption of a single factor of production as the basis of our theory and starting with a given set of resources which may contain any number of factors, we make our assumptions more realistic; and (2) because we are able to derive the same results from a less restrictive set of assumptions, we make our theory more elegant.

The conclusions derived from the labor theory of value hold just as before, and there is no need to restate them here. The only thing we have to remember is that it is not the physical factor cost which determines the value of a commodity, but the opportunities of production of other commodities which have to be foregone in order to produce the particular commodity in question. These opportunity costs will be reflected in the exchange ratios which will prevail between the different commodities.

3. Effects of the Size of Countries

a. Countries of Equal Size

Let us assume first that there are only two countries of equal size. By equal size we shall mean the identity of the *value* of the output of the countries. The value of the output is naturally given by the maximum physical output times the price of the commodity. Expressed geometrically, it means that the production possibility curves of the two countries will just touch (be tangent to) the same price line. In Figure 2-3 we show the production possibility curves for the United Kingdom and the United States. The maximum quantities of cloth and wheat which can be produced are given in Table 2-2.

TABLE 2-2

| | Maximum Outputs of | |
	Cloth or	Wheat
United Kingdom	200	200
United States	100	400

The United Kingdom has a comparative advantage in the production of
cloth, the United States has a comparative advantage in the production of
wheat. The United Kingdom will tend to export cloth and import wheat, while
the United States will tend to export wheat and import cloth. The countries
conform to our initial assumption of equal size *if* the price ratio of cloth to
wheat is two to one. This results in a price line of the slope $-\frac{1}{2}$, which will
pass through both the point of complete specialization of the United Kingdom
in cloth (production takes place at P^{UK}) and complete specialization of the
United States in wheat (production takes place at P^{US}). The countries will

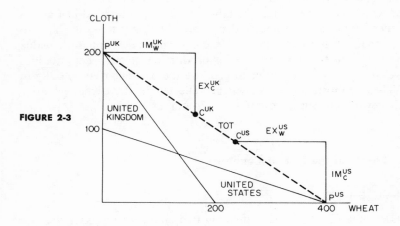

FIGURE 2-3

exchange commodities in the ratio indicated by the price line (dotted line).
Assuming that the countries want to consume the commodity bundles shown
by C^{US} and C^{UK}, we will find the United States exporting EX_W^{US} of wheat and
importing IM_C^{US}. The United Kingdom will trade EX_C^{UK} of cloth for IM_W^{UK}
of wheat. Naturally, there are also different amounts which could be traded,
the only requirement being that the quantities of exports and imports match
exactly for each commodity. The precise quantities of the two commodities
which are consumed in the two countries are not important in determining
the pattern or degree of international specialization. Specialization in both
countries will be complete.

*Under constant cost conditions, countries that are of equal size and have
different relative domestic cost ratios of production will specialize completely*

in the production of the commodity in which they enjoy a comparative cost advantage.

b. Countries of Unequal Size

If the trading countries are of unequal size, i.e., if one country can produce a collection of commodities more valuable than the other country, we have a greater variety of possible outcomes than if the countries are of equal size. In Figure 2-4 we show the production possibility curves of the United Kingdom and the United States respectively. In the pretrade situation, the price line showing the domestic exchange ratio of the two commodities will coincide with the straight line production possibility curve in each country. After trade opens up, a common international exchange ratio for the two commodities will be established. For the international terms of trade to be in equilibrium, the condition of balanced physical trade must be satisfied. One such situation, fulfilling all the conditions given, is depicted in Figure 2-4. The United King-

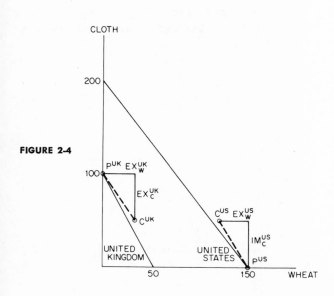

FIGURE 2-4

dom specializes in the production of cloth, producing at point P^{UK}, and exchanges cloth for wheat at the international terms of trade (dotted line). Thus she is able to reach consumption point C^{UK}. A similar situation holds true for the United States, which produces at point P^{US}, and trades wheat for cloth to reach consumption point C^{US}. In this example both countries will specialize in the commodity in which they enjoy a comparative cost advantage, and will trade it for the other commodity in order to reach their desired consumption patterns.

In Section 2-1-b we noted that there exist some absolute limits between which the international terms of trade must lie. These limits are given by the pretrade relative cost ratios, because no country will be willing to exchange commodities internationally at worse terms than it could produce them at home. If one of the countries is very small in relation to the other country, it is entirely possible that even complete specialization on the part of the smaller country in one of the commodities—cloth, for example—will not suffice to satisfy the total world demand for cloth. As a result, we should find that the larger country will continue producing both commodities. It will be importing some cloth from the small country, but will produce a certain amount of cloth domestically in order to satisfy the home demand for this commodity.

In this case the international terms of trade will coincide with the domestic pretrade exchange ratio of the country which continues to produce both commodities after trade is opened. Such a situation is shown in Figure 2-5.

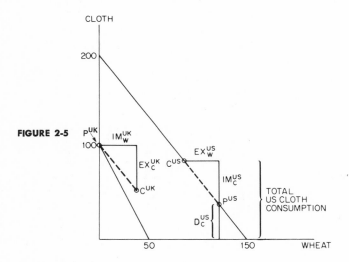

FIGURE 2-5

The United Kingdom (the smaller country of our example) produces at point P^{UK}, specializing completely in the production of cloth. She trades part of her cloth production against wheat imports from the United States, allowing her to consume the commodity combination indicated by C^{UK}. The United States wants to consume at point C^{US}. To achieve this consumption pattern, she imports IM_C^{US} from the United Kingdom, and supplements this with D_C^{US}

produced domestically. The United States thus produces a commodity combination shown by point P^{us}.

The key to much of the understanding of the production patterns that develop in countries of unequal size is found in the fact that the pretrade domestic terms of trade set the limits for the international terms of trade. If after one country has specialized completely in one commodity there is still some excess demand for this commodity, the international terms of trade can no longer change, because the limit to the terms of trade set by the domestic pretrade price ratios has already been reached. Any additional demand that remains at these prices must be satisfied by production under the cost conditions prevailing in the country not yet completely specialized. Therefore, the international terms of trade must necessarily coincide with the slope of the production possibility curve of the country producing both commodities.

If the trading countries are of unequal size and constant costs prevail, international trade will lead to the complete specialization of at least one country. If one country continues to produce both commodities, the international exchange ratio will coincide with the domestic exchange ratio of that country.

4. Effects of Increasing and Decreasing Costs

The analysis so far has been concerned with the special case of constant costs. In the real world we find that such idealized conditions hold only rarely. It is therefore appropriate to extend our analysis to cover both the increasing and decreasing cost cases. Nonlinear production possibility curves may be caused by a variety of different factors. Among the more important are (1) different returns to scale and (2) the existence of factors of production which are specialized in the production of one commodity.

Returns to scale refer to the relationship between inputs and outputs as the scale (or level) of the production process is changed. If a doubling of all inputs leads to a doubling of the outputs, returns to scale are said to be constant; if a doubling of all inputs leads to more than a doubling of all outputs, returns are said to be increasing; and if a doubling of all inputs leads to less than a doubling of the outputs, returns to scale are decreasing. These differences can be caused by factors both inside or outside the firm itself.

Many factors of production are specialized in the production of certain commodities. Such factors are referred to as being product specific. Clearly, any one of these product-specific factors is of relatively less use in the production of other commodities, and we can conclude that the existence of different factor intensities can be responsible for increasing costs in production. The precise way in which different returns to scale and different factor intensities shape the production possibility curve will be investigated further in Chapter 3.

a. Increasing Costs

Increasing costs of production give rise to a production possibility curve which is concave, viewed from the origin. Such a production possibility curve is depicted in Figure 2-6. In this context it is irrelevant whether the costs of production are reckoned in real or opportunity costs. In both cases we will find that the production possibility curve has the bulging shape characteristic of increasing costs.

A country producing any arbitrary combination of commodities described by a point on the production possibility curve will find that as she expands the production of one commodity, the cost of producing this commodity will increase. Figures 2-6 and 2-7 show the production possibility

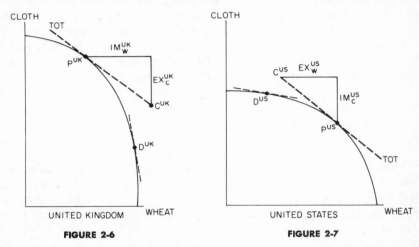

FIGURE 2-6　　　　**FIGURE 2-7**

curves of the United Kingdom and the United States respectively. Before trade opens up, the countries produce all commodities consumed domestically. Possible domestic production and consumption patterns are shown by points D^{UK} and D^{US}. The domestic exchange ratios between cloth and wheat are given by the slopes of the tangents to the production possibility curves at points D^{UK} and D^{US} respectively. After trade opens up, the new international terms of trade will have to lie between the limits established by the domestic exchange ratios. Accordingly, the United Kingdom will tend to produce more cloth (move to production point P^{UK}), while the United States will increase her wheat output (move to production point P^{US}). The United Kingdom will then export some of her cloth in exchange for wheat, moving to consumption point C^{UK}, while the United States will export wheat and import cloth, reaching consumption point C^{US}.

Both countries will specialize, but they will probably *not specialize completely*. This is due to the fact that as the country increases the output of the commodity in which she specializes, her costs of producing this commodity will increase. If costs increase so sharply that the country loses her comparative cost advantage vis-à-vis the other country before complete specialization has taken place, both countries will continue to produce both commodities. If a country reaches the end point of the production possibility curve before the new terms of trade are reached, specialization is naturally complete. We will continue to speak of specialization taking place in the commodity in which the country has a comparative cost advantage, and say that the country will *tend* to export the commodity in which she specializes. Specialization and exchange will again allow the countries concerned to achieve a commodity bundle for consumption which could not have been attained under conditions of autarky.

Countries experiencing increasing cost of production will specialize in the production of the commodity in which they enjoy a comparative cost advantage. The specialization need not be complete.

b. Decreasing Costs

Decreasing costs of production[2] find expression in a production possibility curve which is convex to the origin. Under these conditions there is a multitude of possible outcomes, and we have to restrict our attention to the more important ones.

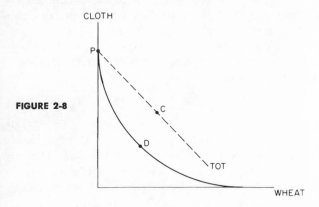

FIGURE 2-8

Figure 2-8 shows the production possibility curve of a country which produces under conditions of decreasing cost. Before specialization, the country can produce any commodity combination located on the production possibility curve, such as D. But, given the possibility of international exchange, the country will specialize in one commodity, say, cloth, produce at point P

---

[2] Note that the economies of scale cannot be due to economies which are internal to the production unit. The existence of internal economies of scale would lead to a breakdown of perfect competition, and monopolistic pricing patterns would evolve which would invalidate some of our results.

on the production possibility curve, and exchange some cloth at the international terms of trade TOT for wheat. Thus she is able to reach consumption point C outside her production possibility curve, which could not have been attained without the possibility of international exchange.[3]

Once specialization in one of the commodities is under way, the country can produce this commodity under conditions of continuously decreasing costs. The decreasing costs per unit will allow this country to outbid the other country to an ever-increasing degree. Thus, once specialization has started, it is likely to continue until it is complete. Initially, a country's specialization in a particular commodity may have been due to historical accident, but once the process has started there is no point of return. This may help to explain the high degree of specialization which we often find in the production of different commodities, where a product becomes associated with the name of the country or region which specializes in its production.

There still exists the possibility that even under these conditions we find one country continuing to produce both commodities. This would be the case if one country, even after complete specialization, were unable to satisfy the total world demand for the commodity in question. The other country would then have to continue producing some of the desired commodity herself, and would thus not be able to take full advantage of the decreasing cost afforded by complete specialization. This case is very similar to the one we encountered in Section 2-3-b when dealing with the effects of differences in country size on specialization patterns under conditions of constant cost.

Countries which experience decreasing cost of production will tend to specialize in production. The specialization will be complete in at least one country, but need not be complete in all countries.

5. Empirical Evidence

Several economists have attempted to test the validity of the elementary form of the comparative cost theory. The most notable attempts were made by G. D. A. MacDougall,[4] Robert Stern,[5] and Bela Balassa.[6] All three inves-

---

[3] Under certain conditions it may be advantageous for a country to specialize completely, even if there is no opportunity for international trade. This will be the case if there is a very strong domestic preference for one of the commodities. This could also occur under conditions of increasing or constant costs of production, though the chances for its occurrence are greater under decreasing cost conditions.

[4] G. D. A. MacDougall, "British and American Exports: A Study Suggested by the Theory of Comparative Costs," *Economic Journal*, December 1951.

[5] R. Stern, "British and American Productivity and Comparative Costs in International Trade," *Oxford Economic Papers*, October 1962.

[6] B. Balassa, "An Empirical Demonstration of Classical Comparative Cost Theory," *Review of Economics and Statistics*, August 1963.

tigators worked with data for the United States and the United Kingdom. MacDougall used 1937, Stern 1950 and 1959, and Balassa 1950 data.

All three investigations try to test the validity of the labor theory of value as the main determinant of international trade. According to this theory, differences in the productivity of labor will result in differences in the cost of production of various commodities, which in turn will affect the pretrade prices for these commodities. If a country has relatively low prices for a commodity, it will tend to export this commodity.

One of the major problems of testing this hypothesis is that we cannot observe the *pretrade prices* which would prevail under conditions of autarky. In the world in which we live countries do trade with each other, and product prices are already equalized (except for differences due to tariffs, transport costs, and the like). Because of this difficulty, we will test directly the hypothesis that the country which has a relatively high productivity of labor in the production of a commodity will tend to export this commodity.

A second problem arises in connection with the tariffs and transport costs which exist in the real world. Especially in 1937, the date of the original study by MacDougall, United States and United Kingdom tariffs were generally high enough to wipe out any comparative cost differences that might have existed. As a result we find that the two countries traded relatively little with each other. For this reason the studies concentrate attention on the export performance of the two countries in *third markets*. In these countries both the United States' and the United Kingdom's products have to overcome the same tariff walls and are faced with often similar transport costs.

Third, a problem arises in the availability of export performance data. For some industries we have *quantity* of export data, while for others only *value* of export data are available. No great difficulties are to be expected from this handicap, since value of exports is nothing but quantity times price of the exported commodity. As both countries are able to obtain the same price in the world market, the two indices should yield the same results.

The theory would predict that the country whose productivity of labor is higher than the other country's in the production of a certain commodity would capture the whole export market for this commodity. The actual results of MacDougall are shown in Figure 2-9, where the productivity of labor ratio is shown on the vertical axis and the export ratio on the horizontal axis. (Both are log scales.) We find that there is an approximately linear relationship between the productivity and export ratios. This shows that in those commodities where the United States labor productivity is the highest (relative to the United Kingdom), the United States will capture the largest share of the export markets. As the relative advantage of the United States falls, the export market share falls, too. We find that the process is continuous in the sense that no one country succeeds in capturing the whole export market as a result of a small comparative cost advantage. This is due to several causes: (1) The

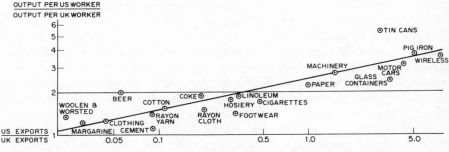

Source: Adapted from G. D. A. MacDougall, "British and American Exports: A Study Suggested by the Theory of Comparative Costs," *Economic Journal*, December 1951, p. 703.

FIGURE 2-9

products shown here are not homogeneous within commodity classes. There are quality and design differences among all the automobile types lumped together in the commodity classification *cars*. Thus product differentiation is one reason no country can capture the whole export market. (2) There are imperfectly competitive markets in the real world. Oligopolistic or monopolistic industries tend to price their products differently than perfectly competitive industries, and these industries are often able to maintain certain markets because of their special pricing techniques. Both reasons mentioned will lead to a continuous distribution of the industries, where high productivity of labor is strongly correlated with a superior export performance.

We need to explain here why the line showing productivity of labor/export performance relationship indicates that the United States' labor productivity must be more than twice the British labor productivity for the former to capture the greater share of the export market. To begin, in 1937 wages in the United States were about *twice* the level of British wages. An American worker would have to be twice as productive as his British colleague if the product were to have the same production costs. This accounts for most of the difference. In addition, there is the question of indirect labor. Indirect labor is the labor spent not in the direct production process of manufacturing the commodity, but in transporting, distributing, and servicing it. It is argued that the amount of such indirect labor, which is not reflected in the productivity data shown here, is greater for the United States than for the United Kingdom. Finally, there is the question of Commonwealth preference, the practice of member countries of the British Commonwealth of Nations granting preferential treatment to commodities produced by member countries. This practice also would tend to discriminate against the United States, requiring her to have a much higher labor productivity than Great Britain before she could capture the greater share of the export market.

The studies by Stern and Balassa for the postwar period confirm and amplify the conclusion reached in the pioneer effort by MacDougall. They found that other factors, such as capital costs per unit of output and the like, did not influence the export performance of the countries to any significant extent. Their results confirmed MacDougall's findings of a high correlation between productivity of labor and export shares.

However, recent work by Jagdish Bhagwati[7] casts some doubt on the seemingly convincing studies cited. Using a somewhat more sophisticated technique, Bhagwati finds that linear regressions of export price ratios (United States/United Kingdom) on labor productivity ratios yield no significant regression coefficients. Similarly, regressions of unit labor costs on export price ratios for the same two countries yield no significant results.

The strong positive results of MacDougall, Balassa, and Stern regarding the usefulness of the classical theory of comparative costs should therefore be regarded with caution until more conclusive evidence becomes available.

SUGGESTED FURTHER READINGS

Balassa, Bela, "An Empirical Demonstration of Classical Comparative Cost Theory," *Review of Economics and Statistics*, August 1963.

Bhagwati, Jagdish, "The Pure Theory of International Trade: A Survey," *Economic Journal*, March 1964, Section I (Theorems in Statics: The Pattern of Trade).

Brandis, Royall, "The Myth of Absolute Advantage," *American Economic Review*, March 1967.

Caves, Richard, *Trade and Economic Structure*. Cambridge: Harvard University Press, 1960, pp. 6–22.

Haberler, Gottfried, "A Survey of International Trade Theory," *Special Papers in International Economics*, No. 1, International Finance Section, Princeton University, 1961, Chapter 2.

———, *The Theory of International Trade*. London: Hodge, 1936, Chapters 10–12.

Johnson, Harry, *Money, Trade, and Economic Growth*. Cambridge: Harvard University Press, 1962, Chapter 2.

MacDougall, Donald, "British and American Exports: A Study Suggested by the Theory of Comparative Costs," *Economic Journal*, December 1951.

Meier, Gerald, "The Theory of Comparative Cost Reconsidered," *Oxford Economic Papers*, June 1949.

Stern, Robert, "British and American Productivity and Comparative Costs in International Trade," *Oxford Economic Papers*, October 1962.

[7] Jagdish Bhagwati, "The Pure Theory of International Trade: A Survey," *Economic Journal*, March 1964.

CHAPTER 3

Production
and International Trade

In the previous chapter we analyzed the effects of cost differences between countries on the pattern of international trade. In the simple case of one factor of production, we showed the relationship between factor inputs and products produced. When we utilized the concept of opportunity costs, we refrained from showing the causes responsible for the shape of the production possibility curve. In this chapter, however, we will look behind the production possibility curve and explain the different factors which determine its shape.

We know that international trade will start whenever the domestic price ratios of different commodities are not the same in the countries under consideration. Differences in production possibility curves for different countries constitute one important reason for these international price differentials which in turn lead to the emergence of international trade. It is therefore of the utmost importance to understand clearly the various factors that are responsible for the shape and position of the production possibility curve.[1]

At the same time we will make our theory more general by introducing a second factor of production. The two factors of production referred to may be any factors or factor bundles. In our examples we will usually refer to them as labor (L) and real capital (K).

To simplify the analysis we will assume throughout this chapter that demand patterns in the two countries under consideration are identical and that all production functions are linear and homogeneous. This assumption enables us to eliminate initially any influence that different demand patterns

---

[1] The reader unfamiliar with production theory is advised to read the appropriate material in the Appendix.

26

might have on the structure of international trade. In the next chapter we will drop this assumption and analyze the effects of different demand patterns on trade.

1. Production Functions and Trade

There are three important conditions of production which will be singled out for treatment in the remainder of this chapter: the effects of differences in returns to scale, factor intensities, and factor endowments.

a. Effects of Returns to Scale

We will start our investigation with the effect of different returns to scale in production on the production possibilities of a country. To isolate the effects of the returns to scale, we will assume that the factor intensities in the production of the two commodities are identical and that the factor endowments of the different countries are identical, too. As a consequence we will find that the Edgeworth Box diagrams for the two countries are of the same size and have a straight diagonal contract curve.

(i) Constant Returns to Scale

A production possibility curve displaying constant returns to scale is shown in Figure 3-1a. The quantities of the two outputs, cloth and wheat, are measured along the axes. The units of output of wheat shown along the horizontal axis are measured in such a way that the point R', denoting the maximum amount of output of wheat on the production possibility curve of Figure 3-1a, is vertically above point R, denoting the same maximum level of wheat output in the Edgeworth Box depicted in Figure 3-1b. Similarly, if all resources are devoted to cloth production, OM' of cloth and no wheat would be produced. Mapping the quantity of cloth produced in the Edgeworth Box diagram would result in point M.

TABLE 3-1

Possible Output Combinations Under Constant Returns to Scale

Point	Cloth	Output of and	Wheat
M	40		0
N	30		25
P	20		50
Q	10		75
R	0		100

It is possible to derive the whole production possibility curve from the contract curve. A decrease in cloth production will free resources for wheat production, allowing for an expansion of this industry and vice versa. Different possible output combinations are given in Table 3-1 and are marked on Figure 3-1.

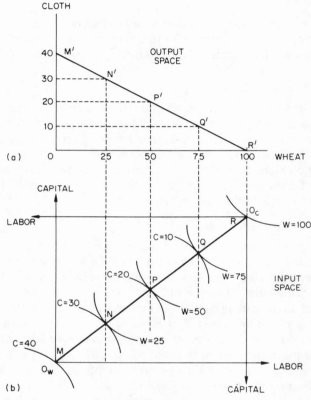

FIGURE 3-1 (a) and (b)

By now it should be clear that for each point on the contract curve there exists one "corresponding" point on the production possibility curve. If factors of production are reallocated between different employments, the output pattern will be changed in the same proportion.

All the points located on the contract curve represent technologically efficient production patterns, just as their corresponding points on the production possibility curve represent technologically efficient production patterns. Similarly, all points in the input space that are not actually located on the contract curve as well as their corresponding points in the output space are technologically inefficient.

Even with constant returns to scale, there may still exist differences in the marginal rate of transformation (shown by the slope of the production possibility curve) in different countries, provided that the returns to scale differ in the sense that one country can produce with the same amount of resources a greater (or smaller) quantity of one of the commodities than the other country. In other words, while the maximum cloth output in both countries may be 40 units, one country may be able to produce 25, 50, 75, and 100 units of wheat, while the other country can produce 20, 40, 60, and 80 units of wheat. Both countries have constant returns to scale, but they differ by a fixed amount.

Countries which have identical factor endowments, identical factor intensities, and are also subject to constant returns to scale may have different production possibility curves if the returns to scale are not identical.

(ii) Decreasing Returns to Scale

We can relax now the assumption of constant returns to scale by allowing decreasing returns to scale in the production of one commodity, say, wheat. The other commodity is still being produced under constant returns to scale, and all other assumptions remain intact. Table 3-2 shows possible output combinations which result from the shifting of equal amounts of resources. Thus, to move from M to N involves the same amount of resource shifting as the movement from N to P, or from P to Q, or from Q to R.

TABLE 3-2

Possible Output Combinations Under Decreasing Returns to Scale in the Production of Wheat

Point	Cloth	Output of and	Wheat
M	40		0
N	30		40
P	20		70
Q	10		90
R	0		100

Note that equal resource shifts will decrease cloth production by 10 units in our example—no matter at which level of output production is already taking place. Wheat production, on the other hand, increases first by 40 units, then by 30, 20, and 10 units. The increments in output due to equal additions of resources become smaller and smaller as the output level increases, i.e., we experience decreasing returns to scale.

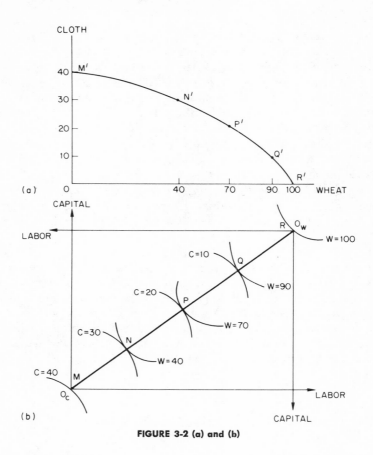

FIGURE 3-2 (a) and (b)

In Figure 3-2 we plot the data supplied in Table 3-2 and find that the production possibility curve is concave, viewed from the origin. Any increase in the production level of one of the two commodities will call for successively larger sacrifices of the other commodity, regardless of whether an expansion is in the production of the commodity which can be produced under decreasing or under constant returns to scale. For *both* commodities the opportunity cost of production increases.

Decreasing returns to scale in one commodity will tend to result in increasing opportunity costs of production for both commodities.

(iii) Increasing Returns to Scale

The case of increasing returns to scale is complementary to the decreasing returns to scale case treated above. Again we will assume that cloth is being produced under constant returns to scale, while wheat is now produced under increasing returns to scale. The data are shown in Table 3-3, and the relevant

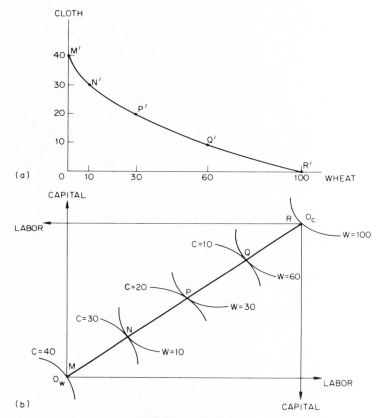

FIGURE 3-3 (a) and (b)

diagrams are drawn in Figure 3-3. The production possibility curve will be convex toward the origin, indicating that the opportunity cost of production decreases.

TABLE 3-3

Possible Output Combinations Under Increasing Returns to Scale in the Production of Wheat

Point	Output of		
	Cloth	and	Wheat
M	40		0
N	30		10
P	20		30
Q	10		60
R	0		100

Increasing returns to scale in one commodity will tend to result in decreasing opportunity costs of production for both commodities.

(iv) The Net Influence of Returns to Scale

Naturally, it is also possible to find various combinations of the three cases described above. Returns to scale may differ in different output ranges of the same commodity, they may differ between commodities, and they may differ between countries. What is important for international trade theory is the *net influence* which returns to scale exercise on the production possibility curve, i.e., the result of the countervailing or reinforcing influences causing different returns to scale. From the fact that there are increasing returns to scale in the production of one commodity, it cannot be inferred that the opportunity costs of production are decreasing. This is because there may be strongly decreasing returns to scale in the other commodity, more than off-setting the mildly increasing returns to scale in the first commodity. The net result would be increasing opportunity costs in the production of both commodities.

If the net influence varies in different output ranges, the opportunity costs of production may be increasing in some ranges of the production possibility curve while decreasing in other ranges. Such a situation is shown in Table 3-4 and Figure 3-4.

TABLE 3-4

Possible Output Combinations Under Varying Returns to Scale

Point	Change in Cloth Output		Total Cloth Output	Total Wheat Output	Change in Wheat Output	
M			40	0		
		3			22	
N	Decreasing		37	22		
	returns	7			21	
P	to scale		30	43		Decreasing
		20			20	returns
Q			10	63		to scale
	Increasing	8			19	
R	returns		2	82		
	to scale	2			18	
S			0	100		

While the production of wheat is subject to mildly decreasing returns to scale throughout the output range, we find that cloth production shows first increasing and then decreasing returns to scale as we move from M to S.

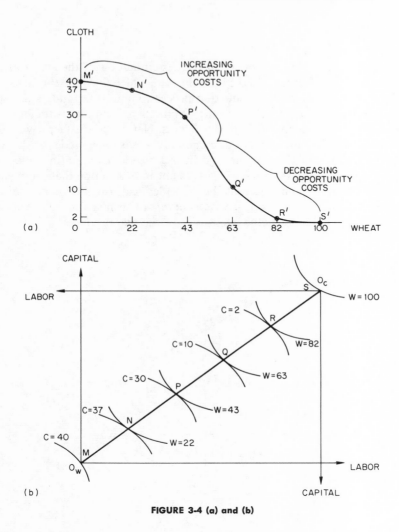

FIGURE 3-4 (a) and (b)

But while the decreasing returns in wheat production are very mild, the increasing returns in cloth production between Q and S are strong enough to predominate. As a result the production possibility curve has a roller coaster shape, exhibiting increasing opportunity costs between M' and P' and decreasing opportunity costs between Q' and S'. The number of different possible combinations is virtually unlimited, and there is nothing that we can say about the direction of trade on a priori grounds. All we know is that whatever commodity can be produced with a comparative cost advantage at home is likely to be exported, while the commodity with the comparative cost disadvantage is likely to be imported.

b. The Effects of Factor Intensities

Another important parameter in the determination of the shape of the production possibility curve is the intensity with which the different factors of production are used in the production process. Quite often inputs are specialized in the production of a specific commodity. Such inputs might be of little use in the production of other products. Naturally, the factor which is specialized in the production of one commodity tends to be used more heavily in the production of this commodity. In order to focus attention solely on the role of the factor intensities, we will assume in this section that production functions are linear homogeneous, but not identical, for both commodities. As a consequence the contract curve is a curve, rather than a straight diagonal line, indicating different factor intensities for the two products.

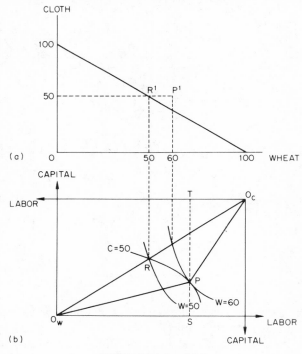

FIGURE 3-5 (a) and (b)

Consider the customary Edgeworth Box diagram shown in Figure 3-5b. Production is thought of as taking place at point P. The quantities of the two inputs devoted to the production of each output are determined by the position of point P. Production of wheat utilizes PS of capital and SO_W of labor, resulting in a relative factor intensity of capital to labor of PS/SO_W. Production of cloth utilizes PT of capital and TO_C of labor, leading to a capital/labor ratio of PT/TO_C. The straight lines drawn from the origins to point P have the slopes PS/SO_W and PT/TO_C respectively. As is evident from the diagram, the ratios PS/SO_W and PT/TO_C are not equal to each other, indicating that there are different factor intensities in the production of the two commodities.

If, instead of using different factor intensities, we insist on operating with *identical* factor intensities in the manufacture of both commodities, production could take place on any point along the *diagonal* $O_W O_C$. Such a point is shown by R in the input space. A mapping of R in the output space would yield point R′, which is located in a straight line production possibility curve. The output levels associated with point R are 50 cloth and 50 wheat.

However, instead of being limited to identical factor intensities, we do have the possibility of utilizing *different* factor intensities. Thus we are able to produce at point P. Point P is located on the same cloth isoquant (cloth = 50) as point R. But P is located on a higher wheat isoquant (wheat = 60) than point R (wheat = 50). All we have to do is to mark the increased wheat output possible in the output space, and with the coordinate supplied by the unchanged cloth output (cloth = 50), we are able to map point P′ in the output space.

It should be pointed out that this mapping procedure from the input to the output space is applicable only to the case of linear homogeneous isoquants, as was initially assumed. The geometry becomes much more complex if we introduce nonlinear returns to scale.

The important result of this exercise is that we can show that point P′ is actually located above the straight line production possibility curve shown in Figure 3-5a. A complete mapping of all points on the contract curve of the Edgeworth Box in the output space would lead to a production possibility curve which is concave, if viewed from the origin. A concave production possibility curve is characterized by increasing opportunity costs of production.

Different factor intensities in the production of several commodities will lead to increasing cost conditions in production. The greater the difference between the factor intensities, the more pronounced will be the curvature of the production possibility curve.

It is possible for the factor intensities to be reversed in different ranges of the production function. Depending on the scale of operations, the commodity being produced may be labor intensive or capital intensive. We might envision a situation where labor intensive methods are used if the total output is relatively small, while capital intensive methods are more economical if the output level increases. Such a situation is shown in Figure 3-6. If production takes place at point P, wheat production is labor intensive and cloth is capital intensive, while the reverse holds true for production at point R. The production possibility curve for this case will typically exhibit the familiar concave shape.

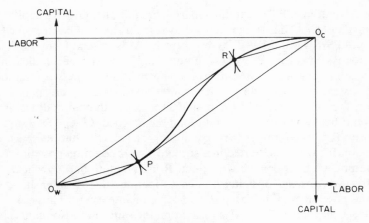

FIGURE 3-6

c. Effects of Factor Endowments

To isolate the effects of factor endowments we will assume that (1) production functions are identical in both countries, (2) all isoquants are linear homogeneous, and (3) the factor intensities are identical for both commodities at any factor price ratio. Thus the only difference between the two countries lies in the relative amounts of factors of production which are available.

Let us assume that the United Kingdom is characterized by the factor endowments shown by the heavily lined box of Figure 3-7b. The contract curve is shown by the diagonal AB, and the corresponding production possibility curve is shown in Figure 3-7b by the line A′B′.

The United States, the second country of our example, is endowed with the same amount of capital as the United Kingdom; thus the height of the box is the same for both countries. Yet the United States has a larger amount of labor than the United Kingdom, which can be shown either as an enlargement of the box to the left (dotted extension) *or* as an enlargement to the right (dashed extension). The two contract curves for the two alternate diagrams are shown by the lines DB and AC. It is clear that the length of the two alternate contract curves is the same. Given our assumption of linear homogeneous isoquants, the commodity combinations that can be produced are also the same under both circumstances. In dealing with the U.S. contract curve AC, we have a set of wheat isoquants common to both countries; the wheat isoquant that goes through point C is the highest for the U.S., but the higher one through B is the highest one for the U.K. The converse is true for cloth, using this time the U.K. contract curve DB. In comparison to the United Kingdom, the United States can produce more of both commodities in exact proportion to the amounts that the United Kingdom can produce.

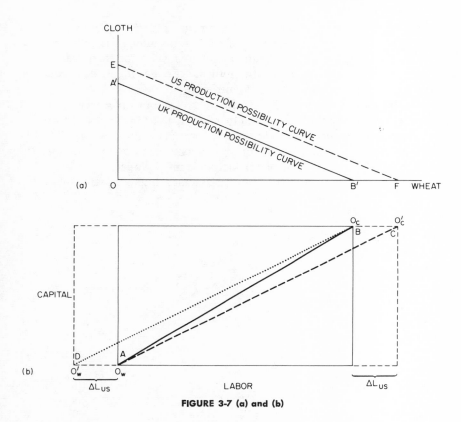

FIGURE 3-7 (a) and (b)

The United States' production possibility curve (EF in Figure 3-7a), therefore, lies parallel to that of the United Kingdom. The comparative cost ratios will be the same in the two countries, thus eliminating the reason for the emergence of international trade, provided taste patterns in the two countries are identical.

If the factor intensities of all products produced by one country are the same, and the same holds true for the other country, then the two countries will not trade with each other even if the factor endowments differ.

d. Different Factor Intensities and Endowments: The Heckscher-Ohlin Theory

One particular constellation of assumptions concerning the differences that exist between countries has received a considerable amount of attention in economics literature. The so-called Heckscher-Ohlin theory[2] of the emer-

---

[2] Eli Heckscher presented the theory first in "The Effects of Foreign Trade on the Distribution of Income," *Economisk Tidskrift*, 1919 (reprinted in H. Ellis and L. Metzler, eds., *Readings in the Theory of International Trade*, Philadelphia, 1950, Chapter 13). This theory was elaborated on by Bertil Ohlin, *International and Inter-regional Trade*, Cambridge, 1933.

gence of trade assumes (1) that countries are characterized by different factor endowments, and (2) that there are different factor intensities between *products*. But the theory assumes that the factor intensities for each product are the same in all countries, as are the returns to scale. Identical production functions are thus assumed for all countries.

It is important to stress that when we talk about differences in factor endowments, we refer to differences in *relative*, not absolute, endowments. Only the factor *proportions* are important for our analysis. A large country may well have the same factor proportions as a small country despite the fact that the absolute amount of her factors is much larger.

As the Heckscher-Ohlin trade model assumes different factor intensities

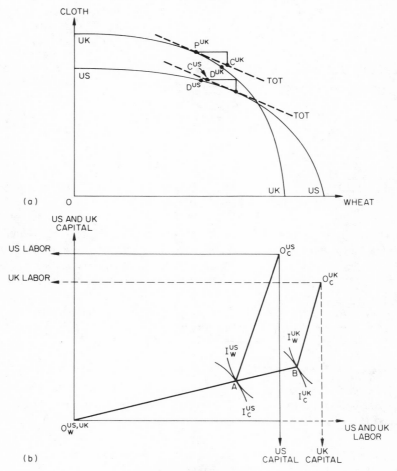

FIGURE 3-8 (a) and (b)

between products and different factor endowments between countries, we will find that the differences between production possibility curves are the *net* result of the influence of these two factors. The different factor intensities between products will be mainly responsible for the degree of *curvature* of the production possibility curve, while the factor endowments are mainly responsible for the *position* of the curve.

Figure 3-8a illustrates the United Kingdom-United States case. The pre-trade domestic production and consumption pattern is indicated by points D^{US} and D^{UK}. The United States is the relatively capital abundant country, while the United Kingdom is relatively labor abundant. From Figure 3-8b we see that wheat production is relatively capital intensive, while cloth production is relatively labor intensive. At each factor price ratio we will find that wheat production utilizes relatively more capital than labor. The country which is relatively abundant in capital, here the United States, can therefore produce relatively more wheat. In the absence of unusually high demand for wheat in the United States, the wheat price will be relatively low in the United States, resulting in a comparative advantage for the United States in wheat production. (Compare the slope of the U.K. production possibility curve at point D^{UK} with the slope of the U.S. production possibility curve at point D^{US}.) After trade opens up we will find that the United States exports wheat.

The reverse holds true for the United Kingdom. The United Kingdom is endowed relatively heavily with labor. Cloth production is relatively labor intensive, thus enabling the United Kingdom to produce relatively more cloth, resulting in a low cloth price, and thus a comparative cost advantage in cloth.

In Figure 3-8a we show also a possible set of international terms of trade. The points of tangency of the production possibility curves with the international terms of trade denote the optimal production patterns P^{US} and P^{UK}. Two possible trade triangles are also shown in the figure, leading to the consumption points C^{US} and C^{UK}.

Given identical production functions but different factor endowments between countries, a country will tend to export the commodity which is relatively (to the other commodity) intensive in her relatively (to the other country) abundant factor.

2. Empirical Evidence

In this section the results of empirical research on the shape of production functions and the effects of factor intensities on patterns of international trade will be presented. We will focus attention on four questions. (1) Are production functions in different countries generally identical? (2) Are production functions characterized by increasing, constant, or decreasing returns to scale? (3) Are factor intensities different in the production of different commodities? And (4) what is the influence of factor endowments on international trade, especially in the general framework of the Heckscher-Ohlin theory?

a. Production Functions

In a celebrated article Arrow, Chenery, Minhas, and Solow[3] (hereafter ACMS) reach the conclusion that production functions between countries are actually different. But they are found to differ only by a constant scale factor. This means that the production function for a commodity, say, automobiles, in the United States differs from the one in the United Kingdom by a fixed percentage. The scale factor will be different from industry to industry, and as a result we find that the production possibility curves for any pair of countries and commodities are different. These different production possibility curves will influence the emerging international trade patterns in the manner discussed above.

b. Returns to Scale

Evidence on returns to scale is available in a large number of econometric studies of cross-section and time-series data of industries and countries. Most of the results of these studies were conveniently summarized by A. Walters.[4] Surveying twenty-two *industry* studies, utilizing cross-section data obtained from individual firms that constitute each industry (excluding agriculture), Walters found that the evidence for *constant* returns to scale is very strong. The same applies to twenty-five studies pertaining to agricultural commodities. In four studies of the production function for individual industries, utilizing time-series estimates, he finds widely different results. Yet in most of these cases the statistical procedure employed is open to serious criticism, and the most that we can say is that the results from time-series industry studies are inconclusive.

In fourteen studies of aggregate production functions for different *countries,* using time series, Walters finds the linearity of the returns to scale remarkably consistent between countries. The same result is found in twenty-eight cross-section studies for countries which utilized industry-wide data. Again, this would add to the evidence in favor of constant returns to scale.

For the *world* as a whole, Earl Thompson[5] finds that nineteen industries studied on a country cross-section basis conform to the constant returns to

[3] K. Arrow, H. Chenery, B. Minhas, and R. Solow, "Capital-Labor Substitution and Economic Efficiency," *Review of Economics and Statistics*, August 1961.

[4] A. A. Walters, "Production and Cost Functions: An Econometric Survey," *Econometrica*, January-April 1963.

[5] E. Thompson, "The Estimation of Returns to Scale with International Cross Section" (unpublished manuscript).

scale hypothesis. This result supports the evidence in favor of constant returns to scale.

c. Factor Intensities

The Walters study also sheds some light on the question of the relative intensity with which different factors of production are used in different industries. Taking data from twenty-two nonagricultural industry studies utilizing individual firm data, and fourteen time-series and twenty-eight cross-section studies for countries utilizing industry-wide data we find that the share of labor coefficient generally varies between .5 and .9, while the share of capital coefficient varies between .1 and .5. In other words, the intensity with which labor and capital are used in production varies widely between different industries. Specialized factors of production, then, should be an important component in the determination of the shape of the production possibility curve in different countries.

d. Factor Endowments and the Heckscher-Ohlin Theory

One of the most widely publicized empirical tests in economics was undertaken by Wassily Leontief [6] in order to examine the validity of the basic Heckscher-Ohlin model of the determination of the structure of international trade. On the basis of the Heckscher-Ohlin theory, one can predict that a country will tend to export the commodity which is relatively (to the other commodity) intensive in the relatively (to the other country) abundant factor.

To test this prediction, Leontief makes use of a 1947 input-output table for the United States. This table gives detailed information on the capital and labor requirements for the production of any commodity group. Since such a table was available for the United States only, Leontief had to resort to the United States import-competing industries to estimate the capital and labor requirements for the production of a given batch of imports rather than using the corresponding requirements in the country of origin as a basis for comparison. This procedure is legitimate only if production functions in the United States and abroad are identical. This is an assumption which the Heckscher-Ohlin theory makes in its most rudimentary form. Products that are not produced in the United States, such as coffee, tea, and jute, are excluded. The same is true of service industries which do not enter into international trade, like trucking, railroad transportation, warehousing, retail trade, banking, etc. Also, it must be assumed that the composition of exports and imports stays constant over the range of variations studied.

Leontief then computes the capital and labor requirements for the pro-

---

[6] W. Leontief, "Domestic Production and Foreign Trade: The American Capital Position Re-examined," *Proceedings of the American Philosophical Society*, September 1953.

duction of $1 million worth of United States exports and import-competing commodities. The results are summarized in Table 3-5.

TABLE 3-5

Domestic Capital and Labor Requirements for Production of $1 Million U.S. Exports and Imports

	Exports	Imports
Capital (1947 prices)	$2,550,780	$3,091,339
Labor (man-years)	182	170
Capital	$13,991	$18,184
Labor	man-year	man-year

Source: W. Leontief, "Domestic Production and Foreign Trade," *Proceedings of the American Philosophical Society*, September 1953. With permission of the author and publisher.

The United States is generally acknowledged to be the most capital abundant country in the world. Consequently, the Heckscher-Ohlin theory predicts that the United States will tend to export commodities which are intensive in her abundant factor, namely, capital, while importing commodities which could be produced at home only by the intensive utilization of her scarce factor of production, labor. The Leontief results contradict this prediction, however, because the United States is shown to export commodities which use only $13,991 of capital per man-year of labor, while importing commodities which require $18,184 of capital per man-year. The data could be interpreted to show that the United States tries to economize on the factor of production capital by trading internationally. These statistics seem to indicate that the Heckscher-Ohlin theory does not yield satisfactory predictions about the direction of trade in this particular case.

Leontief-type tests have been conducted for a number of other countries. R. Bharadwaj[7] found that India tends to export labor-intensive and import capital-intensive commodities. However, in trading with the United States, the most capital abundant country, India is found to export capital-intensive commodities to the United States while importing labor-intensive commodities in return.

M. Tatemoto and S. Ichimura[8] found that Japan, whose main economic

[7] R. Bharadwaj, *Structural Basis for India's Foreign Trade*, Bombay, 1962, and "Factor Proportions and the Structure of Indo-U.S. Trade," *Indian Economic Journal*, October 1962.

[8] M. Tatemoto and S. Ichimura, "Factor Proportions and Foreign Trade: The Case of Japan," *Review of Economics and Statistics*, November 1959.

problem for decades has been her excess population, exports capital-intensive commodities to the rest of the world, while importing labor-intensive commodities. However, this pattern is reversed for trade between Japan and the United States alone, where Japan is shown to export labor-intensive commodities.

In the case of Canada, D. F. Wahl[9] found that Canadian exports are capital intensive and imports labor intensive. As most of Canada's trade is with the United States, this is contrary to what would be expected on the basis of pure theory.

Finally, W. Stolper and K. Roskamp[10] have investigated the nature of East German exports and imports. Compared to the rest of Eastern Europe, East Germany may be considered capital abundant. It was found that her exports are capital intensive and her imports labor intensive.

Of all the empirical studies undertaken, only the cases of direct trade between Japan and the United States and between East Germany and Eastern Europe can be taken to confirm the predictions of the Heckscher-Ohlin theory. In all other studies we find that the empirical evidence contradicts the predictions based on the most elementary version of the theory. We can conclude that in its simplest form the Heckscher-Ohlin theory is not supported by empirical evidence.

It should be noted here that much criticism can be leveled against the tests referred to. Many other factors determining the direction of trade can be allowed for in more complete models, based on the simple Heckscher-Ohlin model discussed here. These more sophisticated arguments will be taken up in Section 5-6.

SUGGESTED FURTHER READINGS

Arrow, K., H. Chenery, B. Minhas, and R. Solow, "Capital-Labor Substitution and Economic Efficiency," *Review of Economics and Statistics*, August 1961.

Caves, Richard, *Trade and Economic Structure*. Cambridge: Harvard University Press, 1960, pp. 23–36 and Chapter 6.

Corden, Max, "Recent Developments in the Theory of International Trade," *Special Papers in International Economics*, No. 7, International Finance Section, Princeton University, 1965, Chapter 2.

Haberler, Gottfried, "A Survey of International Trade Theory," *Special Papers in International Economics*, No. 1, International Finance Section, Princeton University, 1961, Chapter 3.

[9] D. F. Wahl, "Capital and Labour Requirements for Canada's Foreign Trade," *Canadian Journal of Economics and Political Science*, August 1961.
[10] W. Stolper and K. Roskamp, "Input-Output Table for East Germany with Applications to Foreign Trade," *Bulletin of the Oxford Institute of Statistics*, November 1961.

Heckscher, Eli, "The Effects of Foreign Trade on the Distribution of Income," *Economisk Tidskrift*, 1919 (reprinted in H. Ellis and L. Metzler, *Readings in the Theory of International Trade*, Philadelphia, 1949, Chapter 13).

Leontief, Wassily, "Domestic Production and Foreign Trade: The American Capital Position Re-examined," *Proceedings of the American Philosophical Society*, September 1953.

Lerner, Abba, "The Diagrammatical Representation of Cost Conditions in International Trade," *Economica*, August 1932.

Ohlin, Bertil, *International and Inter-regional Trade*. Cambridge: Harvard University Press, 1933.

Rybczyniski, T. M., "Factor Endowment and Relative Commodity Prices," *Economica*, November 1955.

Savosnick, Kurt, "The Box Diagram and the Production Possibility Curve," *Economisk Tidskrift*, 1958.

Vanek, Jaroslav, *International Trade: Theory and Economic Policy*. Homewood, Ill.: Richard D. Irwin, 1962, pp. 186–198.

Walters, Alan, "Production and Cost Functions: An Econometric Survey," *Econometrica*, January/April 1963.

CHAPTER 4

Consumption
and International Trade

Preference patterns can be expressed by the graphical technique of indifference curves, whose nature and properties are discussed in the Appendix. It will suffice here to say that an indifference curve is defined as the collection of all commodity combinations which will yield the same amount of satisfaction or utility to the consumer.

Indifference curves are defined for individual persons, and our first problem is to derive an aggregate indifference curve for all residents of a given country, often referred to as a *community indifference curve*. Such a community indifference curve may then be used to represent the preference patterns for the country as a whole, and will also allow us to draw certain welfare conclusions if the country moves from one community indifference curve to another. As the community indifference curve is to be used for these important purposes, it is imperative that we scrutinize carefully its derivation and theoretical foundation.

1. Community Indifference Curves

a. Derivation of Community Indifference Curves

In deriving the community indifference curves from the indifference curve maps of individual consumers, we will start the analysis with the case of two consumers. This can be extended afterward to cover any number of individuals.

Figure 4-1 shows the indifference curve set for Mr. A in its customary position. Quantities of the two commodities cloth and wheat are measured along the two axes. Superimposed on the diagram is Mr. B's coordinate

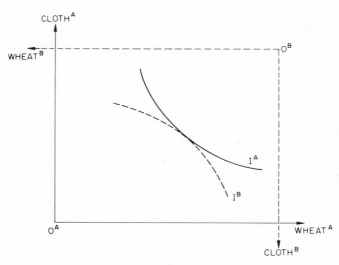

FIGURE 4-1

system and indifference curve set (broken lines), but it is drawn upside down and the sides are reversed. Cloth for Mr. B is measured along the vertical axis, but in the downward direction; wheat is measured along the horizontal axis, in the leftward direction.

Now we arbitrarily pick two indifference curves which are tangent to each other, one for each consumer. Two such indifference curves might be I^A and I^B. At any point along one of these indifference curves, the consumer experiences a constant level of utility. It does not matter *where* the two curves are tangent to each other—the only important consideration is that they are tangent to each other. The tangency condition assures that no reallocation of resources could make one person better off without making the other one worse off. As far as the distribution of a given bundle of goods is concerned, the point of tangency represents an optimum.

It is now possible to slide the two indifference curves along each other in such a manner that the two coordinate systems always stay parallel to each other. This is done in Figure 4-2. The origin of Mr. A's coordinate system, O^A, stays constant throughout this procedure. Initially, the origin for Mr. B's coordinate system is located at O^B_P. Both persons consume quantities of cloth and wheat shown by point M, which is located on I^A and I^B_P respectively. Now we can move Mr. B's coordinate system and the indifference map belonging to it down and to the right. During this process we are careful to keep the two indifference curves I^A and I^B in a constant tangency position. One such new tangency position is shown by point N. At N both consumers are still on the same indifference curve as at M; however, the respective quantities of cloth and wheat consumed by each one of the persons has changed.

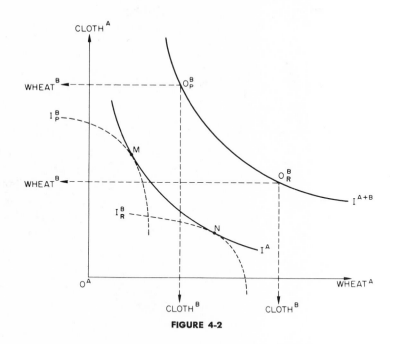

FIGURE 4-2

The *aggregate* quantities of cloth and wheat which both persons consume together is indicated by the respective points O^B with reference to the origin O^A. The moving point O^B (O_P^B, O_R^B, etc.) generates a path which shows the cloth/wheat combinations that are required to keep each one of the consumers on the same indifference curve. As each consumer individually stays on the same indifference curve during the process, the points generated by the moving origin describe commodity combinations between which the two consumers together are indifferent. The collection of commodity combinations between which the consumers together are indifferent defines the *community indifference curve* (CIC) for these two consumers. This construct is the community indifference curve we intended to derive.

We can also draw some inferences about the *slope* of the community indifference curve. The slopes of the two individual indifference curves are equal to each other at point M (Figure 4-2). The marginal rates of substitution of cloth for wheat are the same for both the consumers individually and, therefore, they should also be the same as the rate for the two consumers together. Thus the slope of the community indifference curve of Mr. A and Mr. B at point O_P^B should be the same as the slope of the individual indifference curves at M. The same holds true for the slope of the community indifference curve at O_R^B and the individual indifference curves at N.

We are able to extend this analysis to any number of persons by sliding

Mr. C's indifference curves along the community indifference curve for Mr. A and Mr. B. Any desired number of individual indifference curves can be added in this fashion.

A community indifference curve depicts all commodity combinations that will yield constant utility to the members of the community—individually and together.

b. Problems Associated with Community Indifference Curves

In Figure 4-3 we show two indifference curves which are tangent at point L. By sliding the indifference curves I_0^B and I_1^A along each other we generate the community indifference curve CIC_L. If we had picked instead the two indifference curves through point M, I_0^A and I_1^B, we would have generated the different community indifference curve CIC_M. Note that the initial total endowment of cloth and wheat is the same in both cases; the only difference is the *distribution* of cloth and wheat between Mr. A and Mr. B. It is easily seen that because the slope of the common tangency of the two indifference curves at L is different from the one at M, the community indifference curves corresponding to the two income distributions have different slopes. More community indifference curves through point O^B with still different slopes

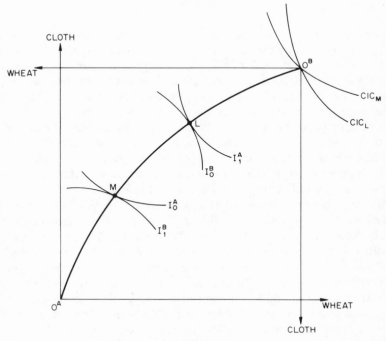

FIGURE 4-3

can be generated by changing the income distribution anywhere along the contract curve $O^A MLO^B$.

We are able to derive by this method an infinite number of community indifference curves through point O^B. This, however, leads to an inconsistency. On the one hand, we can say that a commodity combination represented by point O^B will yield a certain level of welfare; on the other hand, we have different indifference curves through this point, and different indifference curves denote different levels of welfare. Only one of these two propositions can be true. Our results imply that changes in income distribution will lead to different community indifference curves, or that the community indifference map is *not* independent of the income distribution within the community.

The dependence of the community indifference curve on the society's income distribution is explained by the fact that the utility measure used is *ordinal*. Ordinal utility allows only for "better than" or "worse than" comparisons, but does not permit any statement of the numerical size of the utility gains or losses. Thus it is impossible to judge the net effect on society's utility level of a change which is due to an improvement in one person's utility and is accompanied by a decrease in another person's utility. This limitation of the analysis can cause community indifference curves to be inconsistent.

c. Justifications for Community Indifference Curves

Due to the importance of community indifference curves in analyzing the determination of equilibrium in international trade, as well as for deriving welfare conclusions about the effects of free and restricted trade, it is worthwhile to make an effort to salvage the concept of community indifference curves for economic theory. There are various sets of assumptions which will permit the derivation of uniquely determined community indifference curves. Although all justifications presented are objectionable on certain grounds, it is still possible to see how closely the assumptions are actually approximated by real world conditions.

(i) One Inhabitant

The simplest and most trivial justification of community indifference curves is that the entire population of the country in question is composed of a single individual. Robinson Crusoe on his island might serve as an illustration.

(ii) Benevolent Dictator

If there exists a benevolent dictator whose decisions reflect the preferences of the population, he may define a single set of communal preferences. This uniquely defined preference set would have all the properties that individual preference sets have.

(iii) Same Incomes and Tastes

If all residents of the country have the same taste patterns and income levels, we are able to derive a single set of nonintersecting community indifference curves. The assumption of identical tastes is not altogether unreasonable, considering the general conformity created by the similarity of climate and cultural patterns that prevail among the residents of the same country. The assumption of identical incomes assures that all individuals are actually able to attain the same indifference curve. This can be achieved only through a completely egalitarian distribution. Specifying the income distribution excludes the possibility of intersecting community indifference curves. Furthermore, it means that the community indifference curves are nothing but a blown-up version of the individual indifference curves.

(iv) Same Tastes and Homogeneous Indifference Curves

The assumption of identical taste patterns and homogeneous[1] indifference curves would also allow us to draw up nonintersecting community indifference curves. The identical tastes assumption has already been discussed under (iii) above.

Homogeneous indifference curves are characterized by the fact that consumers, confronted with a certain set of relative prices, will buy the same proportion of the commodities irrespective of their income level. The combination of the two assumptions assures that the contract curve in the Edgeworth Box diagram showing two consumers will always be a diagonal straight line. Because of the homogeneity assumption, all marginal rates of substitution along the contract curve are the same, irrespective of income distribution. It follows that the slope of the community indifference curve is uniquely determined. Intersecting community indifference curves are thus ruled out.

(v) Same Incomes and Homogeneous Indifference Curves

Also, if all individuals have the same incomes and homogeneous though not necessarily identical indifference curves, the resulting set of community indifference curves is unique. We have, therefore, again succeeded in eliminating the problem of changing income distributions, which resulted in intersecting community indifference curves.

To summarize: Sections (iii) through (v) showed that *any two* of the following three conditions will yield uniquely determined community indifference curves: identical tastes, identical incomes, or homogeneous indifference curves.

---

[1] For the definition of homogeneity see Appendix.

(vi) Optimal Income Redistribution

There is one other assumption which will allow us to justify the use of community indifference curves: it requires that the social utility of the last dollar of income be the same for all individuals. National income is distributed so that no reallocation of earnings could increase the recipient's welfare by more than it would decrease the welfare of individuals losing these earnings. From the standpoint of society as a whole, income would be distributed in an optimal fashion because everybody derives the same marginal benefit from the last dollar he earns. Any deviation from the socially optimal income distribution has to be corrected by compensation payments by the gainers to the losers. The aggregate level of utility for society as a whole is not changed, because gainers are always compensating losers, and the original utility level can be maintained. The compensation payments assure that we move along one community indifference curve independent of the income distribution.

2. Consumption Patterns and International Trade

In this section we will investigate the effects of different consumption patterns on international trade. To isolate the role of consumption we will assume throughout that the conditions of production are identical in all countries concerned. This assumption will be relaxed in Chapter 5, where we will analyze the conditions of general equilibrium.

a. Direction of Trade

A country in isolation has to produce all the commodities she wants to consume herself. The optimal commodity combination is defined by the condition of equality of the marginal rates of substitution in consumption and the marginal rates of transformation in production for all commodity pairs. The equilibrium domestic exchange ratio is given by the slope of the tangent at the point at which the highest community indifference curve touches the production possibility curve. (For a more detailed review see Appendix.) Such a point of domestic equilibrium is given by point D in Figure 4-4, and the exchange ratio is shown by the slope of the line TOT_D.

If the country has the option of trading internationally at a given international exchange ratio (terms of trade) TOT_I, she will rearrange her consumption and production patterns accordingly. At this juncture we are not concerned with the determination of the international terms of trade themselves, and we will simply assume that they are given to the country.

The optimal production pattern for the country is attained when the marginal rate of transformation in production is equal to the international terms of trade. Under these conditions the country produces a commodity bundle which has the maximum possible value in international markets. Such an optimal production point, given the terms of trade TOT_I, is shown by point P in Figure 4-4. The possibility of trade at the international terms of

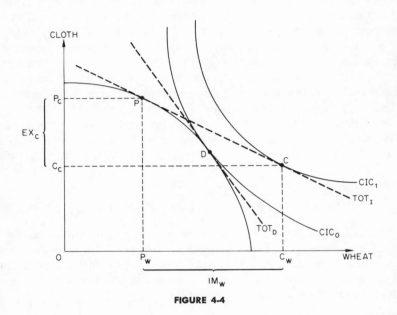

FIGURE 4-4

trade will allow the country to modify the commodity bundle that it produces to suit domestic consumption patterns by exchanging some of the commodities produced against other commodities. Thus it is no longer necessary for the production pattern to coincide with the consumption pattern. The country will alter the composition of her commodity bundle until the highest possible community indifference curve is reached, thereby attaining the greatest possible level of utility for the residents of the country. This condition is fulfilled when the marginal rate of substitution in consumption is equal to the international terms of trade. The community indifference curve CIC_1 is tangent at this point (point C in Figure 4-4) to the international terms of trade line TOT_I.

The modification of the commodity bundle produced (point P) into the commodity bundle consumed (point C) involves international exchange. The country will produce P_C of cloth, and consume only C_C of it. It will also produce P_W of wheat, yet want to consume C_W. In order to maintain the optimal production and consumption patterns, the country must export $P_C - C_C$ of cloth in return for which it receives $C_W - P_W$ of wheat imports.

Excluding the possibility of a Giffen good,[2] a country will tend to import (export) the commodity which has become cheaper (more expensive) in relation to the other commodity after the new international exchange ratio has been established.

b. Determination of International Prices

To show the determination of the international exchange ratio we have to introduce a second country into our analysis. The two countries are assumed to have identical production possibility curves and different demand patterns. Two such countries, the United States and the United Kingdom, are depicted in Figure 4-5. The United States is shown to have a preference

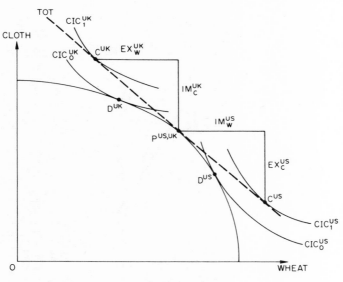

FIGURE 4-5

for wheat while the United Kingdom prefers cloth. After trade opens up, the two countries will both produce at the same point on the production possibility curve, no matter what the consumption pattern. This is due to the fact that international exchange will result in a common set of terms of trade, represented by the line TOT. As the two production possibility curves are identical, they can be tangent to the international terms of trade only at the same point. This point is the production point for both countries and is shown as point $P^{US,UK}$ on the graph.

---

[2] A Giffen good is a commodity whose quantity demanded varies *directly* with the price.

However, the two countries have different preference patterns, and the community indifference curves will therefore be tangent to the international terms of trade line at different points. Two possible equilibrium consumption points are shown by points C^{US} and C^{UK}.

If the terms of trade are to be equilibrium terms of trade, international trade must be balanced, meaning that the quantity of wheat which the United States wants to import must be exactly equal to the quantity of wheat that the United Kingdom wants to export. The reverse must hold true for cloth. Unless these conditions are met, there will be forces set up which will tend to change the international terms of trade until equilibrium is restored.

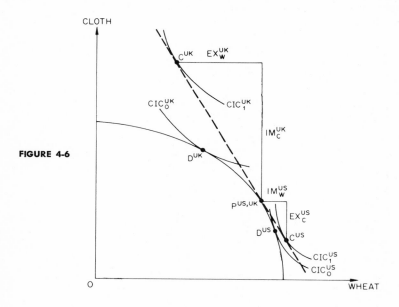

FIGURE 4-6

Such a disequilibrium situation is shown in Figure 4-6. Here the quantity of cloth imports demanded by Britain exceeds the quantity of cloth exports supplied by the United States at the prevailing terms of trade. The reverse applies to wheat. There will be an excess demand for cloth and an excess supply of wheat. As a consequence, the price of cloth will tend to rise while the price of wheat will tend to fall. Thus a smaller quantity of cloth will exchange for a given quantity of wheat. In the graph this price change would be represented by a counterclockwise rotation of the terms of trade line. The rotation will continue until all excess demands and supplies are eliminated, meaning that equilibrium has been restored.

In equilibrium the following conditions are fulfilled: (1) the marginal rate of substitution and the marginal rate of transformation are both equal to the international terms of trade, and (2) the quantities of the commodities traded are equal to each other.

Trade will emerge when, irrespective of production costs, the domestic price ratios are different. A country will export (import) the commodity which is, relative to the other commodity, cheaper (more expensive) at home than abroad.

c. The Offer Curve

The construction of the equilibrium terms of trade presented in the previous section is rather cumbersome since it involves the constant adjustment of the terms of trade until a position is reached where the quantities traded balance. It is convenient to introduce here a tool of analysis which will allow us to determine the equilibrium terms of trade more directly and with greater precision. Since in this chapter we focus attention on the effects of consump-

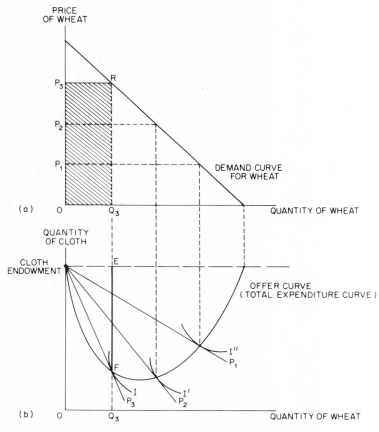

FIGURE 4-7 (a) and (b)

tion patterns on international trade, we will assume that each country is endowed with a certain fixed commodity combination. The way in which this initial commodity combination is obtained is of no immediate interest to us.

Figure 4-7a shows the familiar demand curve for wheat. Given the price P_3, people will demand the quantity Q_3. The total expenditures on the commodity are shown by the crosshatched area OP_3RQ_3. If there are only two commodities, this means that this country is willing to spend (or offer) OP_3RQ_3 of cloth for wheat. This information can also be seen in the lower part of the diagram.

In Figure 4-7b we show the quantity of cloth along the vertical axis and the quantity of wheat along the horizontal axis. Given the price of wheat (in terms of cloth) indicated by the price line P_3, the country will be willing to give up EF of cloth in exchange for OQ_3 of wheat. The *area* OP_3RQ_3 in Figure 4-7a is equal to the *distance* EF in Figure 4-7b.

Note that point F is depicted as an equilibrium point, given the price line P_3. This must mean, however, that a wheat/cloth indifference curve (indifference curve I in Figure 4-7b) is tangent to the price line at point F. Only then would point F be the most preferred point anywhere along P_3.

Similarly, given any other price of wheat, such as P_1 or P_2, we are able to find the quantity of wheat demanded at that price and the quantity of cloth offered in exchange. Given any price ratio, the amounts of cloth offered in exchange for wheat delineate the *offer curve* for the country in question. The offer curve may also be described as the line connecting all points at which an indifference curve is tangent to a price line.

d. Offer Curves and International Price Determination

To show the determination of the terms of trade between two trading partners, we must reintroduce the United Kingdom into our analysis.

In Figure 4-8 we reproduce the offer curve diagram from Figure 4-7b for the United States. In the same figure we also show the offer curve diagram for the United Kingdom, but it is shown upside down and with the sides reversed. The origin for the United Kingdom's coordinate system is labeled O^{UK}, wheat is measured in the horizontal direction to the left, and cloth in the vertical direction downward. The United Kingdom's offer curve is labeled OC^{UK}.

Note that the United States has an initial cloth endowment of AO^{US}, while the United Kingdom has an initial wheat endowment of AO^{UK}. Both countries are willing to modify their initial commodity bundle by exchanging any commodity combination that is located on their offer curve. By trading, they try to reach the highest possible community indifference curve for each country.

Among all the points on the offer curves for the United Kingdom and the

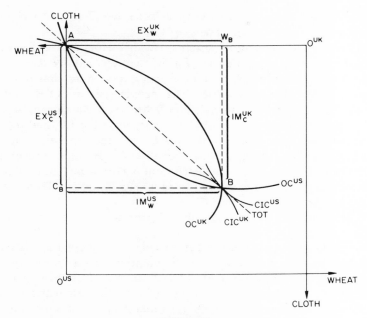

FIGURE 4-8

United States, there is only one point at which the quantities which the two countries want to exchange are consistent with each other. This is the point of intersection of the two offer curves: point B. This point determines the terms of trade TOT. The United States wants to export AC_B of cloth in exchange for BC_B of wheat, while the United Kingdom wants to export AW_B of wheat in exchange for BW_B of cloth. The quantities that the two countries wish to exchange at this set of terms of trade match exactly, and the international markets will be cleared at this price ratio.

Any other terms of trade line will lead to surpluses or shortages in international markets, and market forces will tend to restore equilibrium. A detailed discussion of the stability of equilibrium is deferred to Section 5-3-c.

The intersection of the offer curves of the two countries determines the equilibrium terms of trade. The quantities of the two commodities that the countries wish to exchange will match exactly.

3. Empirical Evidence

In this chapter we have demonstrated how different demand patterns in different countries can theoretically constitute a cause for the emergence of international trade, even if the production possibilities of the countries involved are identical. Consequently, it is important to know whether demand patterns in different countries tend to be sufficiently different to account for the emergence of international trade.

In his survey of expenditure patterns, Hendrik Houthakker[3] found that the income elasticities of the demand for different commodity classes—such as food, clothing, housing, and other expenditures—were similar but not identical between different countries. The income elasticities for food consumption ranged generally between .3 and .7; those for clothing, between 1.0 and 1.5; those for housing were usually slightly less than 1.0; and those for other expenditures were generally above 1.4. Thus the expenditure patterns in different countries varied, but the variation is—perhaps surprisingly— small. National differences in climate, cultural patterns, and social organization are apparently not large enough to cause significantly different income elasticities between countries.

Within the same country, expenditure patterns were found to be very similar.

Other studies[4] of expenditure patterns shed more light on the relationship between income and expenditures on consumption. It was generally found that the percentage of food expenditures declines as the income level goes up. A semilogarithmic function seems to explain the relationship between income and food expenditures rather well. On the other hand, most other commodities are best characterized by a double-logarithmic function.

While it is true that income *elasticities* do not vary greatly between countries, we can conclude that countries with widely different per capita income *levels* will typically exhibit dissimilar demand patterns. In addition, demand will be a fairly important factor in the determination of the structure of international trade between countries with different per capita income levels, while for countries with similar per capita income levels it will be of minor importance. Of course, demand is only one factor determining the direction of trade. Several other important magnitudes are discussed in Chapters 2 and 3.

SUGGESTED FURTHER READINGS

Baumol, William, "The Community Indifference Map," *Review of Economic Studies*, 1949–50.

Caves, Richard, *Trade and Economic Structure*. Cambridge: Harvard University Press, 1960, Chapter 7.

[3] H. S. Houthakker, "An International Comparison of Household Expenditure Patterns, Commemorating the Centenary of Engel's Law," *Econometrica*, October 1957.

[4] S. J. Prais and H. S. Houthakker, *The Analysis of Family Budgets*, Cambridge, 1955.

Houthakker, Hendrik, "An International Comparison of Household Expenditure Patterns," *Econometrica*, October 1957.

Leontief, Wassily, "The Use of Indifference Curves in the Analysis of Foreign Trade," *Quarterly Journal of Economics*, May 1933 (reprinted in H. Ellis and L. Metzler, *Readings in the Theory of International Trade*, Homewood, Ill.: Richard D. Irwin, 1955, Chapter 10).

Lerner, Abba, "The Diagrammatical Representation of Demand Conditions in International Trade," *Economica*, August 1934.

Samuelson, Paul, "Social Indifference Curves," *Quarterly Journal of Economics*, February 1956.

Vanek, Jaroslav, *International Trade: Theory and Economic Policy*, Homewood, Ill.: Richard D. Irwin, 1962, Chapter 13.

CHAPTER 5

Equilibrium
in International Trade

In this chapter we will consider the interaction of the different variables that were discussed in the previous chapters in determining international equilibrium. The analysis of the previous chapters was limited in the sense that we were holding constant some of the variables affecting international equilibrium in order to allow us to analyze the influence of the other variables step by step. We are now ready to assemble the individual building blocks and to analyze the model in general equilibrium terms, considering the interaction of all the variables at once.

1. Consumption, Production, and International Trade

In countries where there are differences *both* in consumption and cost patterns among commodities, it is possible that demand patterns tend to make one commodity the export commodity, while production cost patterns tend to make the other commodity the export commodity. Which of the two commodities will actually be exported and which will be imported will depend on the relative strength of the effects. Naturally, it is also possible for the two effects to work in the same direction, thus reinforcing each other. The net result cannot be predicted from either the community indifference curves or the production possibility curves for the two countries in isolation.

In Figure 5-1 we show the production possibility curves for both the United Kingdom and the United States. Only the final equilibrium situation is shown, where the United Kingdom consumes and produces at points C^{UK} and P^{UK} respectively, while the United States is at points C^{US} and P^{US}. The

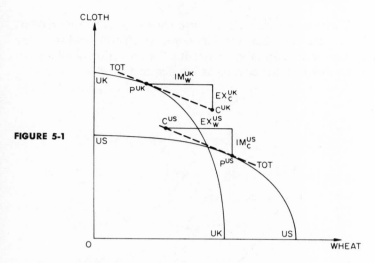

FIGURE 5-1

amounts traded are indicated by the vertical and horizontal differences between the consumption and production points for each of the two countries. The international terms of trade are shown tangent to the production possibility curve and an indifference curve for each country. The terms of trade lines are parallel, indicating that one common world exchange ratio has been established.

The construction employed is rather cumbersome, and it takes a lot of trying before a set of equilibrium terms of trade can be found at which the quantities that the two countries wish to export and import match exactly. Our next task, therefore, will be to adapt the offer curve technique to the problem of general equilibrium in international markets. This will allow us to condense the relevant information contained in the community indifference curves and the production possibility curve.

2. The International Trade Offer Curve

To derive a technique allowing us to depict the various amounts of international trade that a country is willing to undertake at different terms of trade, we must first find the foreign trade indifference curves for the country concerned.

a. The Trade Indifference Curve

The tool which will enable us to summarize some of the information contained in the domestic community indifference curves and production possibility curves, as far as their relevance for international trade is concerned, he *foreign trade indifference curve*. This curve shows the different amounts of foreign trade, i.e., export-import combinations, which will yield the same level of utility to one country. In other words, it is the collection of all foreign trade combinations to which the country is indifferent.

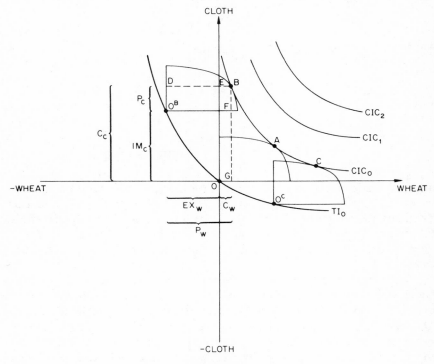

FIGURE 5-2

In Figure 5-2 we show the coordinate system for the country under consideration. In the horizontal direction we measure quantities of wheat, with points to the left of the origin indicating negative quantities of wheat. Similarly, the vertical axis measures quantities of cloth, with points below the origin indicating negative quantities. A set of community indifference curves is drawn in the customary position in the northeastern quadrant. The production possibility curve is also shown, and is tangent to the highest possible community indifference curve at point A, which describes the production and consumption pattern for the country in isolation.

Now it is possible to slide the production possibility curve along the community indifference curve CIC_0 so that the country will remain on the utility level it is able to reach in isolation. This is done in such a fashion that the production possibility curve always stays tangent to the community in-difference curve CIC_0. Note, too, that the coordinate system with reference to which the production possibility curve is drawn is shifted together with the production possibility curve. The points A, B, and C in Figure 5-2 are points of tangency between the sliding production possibility curve and the community indifference curve CIC_0. It is important to keep the coordinates of the shifting production possibility curve always parallel to the original coordinate system.

Let us single out one possible position of the production possibility curve and analyze the production, consumption, and trade patterns which it implies. If the production possibility curve is tangent to the community indifference curve CIC_0 at point B, the country will consume OG of wheat and OE of cloth. Note that all quantities *produced* are measured with reference to the *new origin* of the production possibility curve, namely, point O^B. The country produces now DB of wheat and BF of cloth. It is clear that the country produces too large a quantity of wheat and too small a quantity of cloth to reconcile production and consumption. As consumption and production are not identical, this country will have to engage in foreign trade to make her consumption and production patterns consistent. This adjustment can be accomplished by exporting DE of wheat and importing FG of cloth in exchange. Note that the wheat exports are measured in the negative direction, indicating that we give up this commodity, while the cloth imports are measured in the positive direction, indicating that we supplement our domestic production by imports. As the points A, B, and C lie on the same indifference curve as point P, the country is indifferent between the three positions.

By sliding the production possibility curve along the community indifference curve CIC_0, we are now able to generate a whole series of points (O^C, O, and O^B) which show combinations of exports and imports between which the country is indifferent in the sense that all of them will enable the country to reach the same utility level. The line connecting all points of indifference between different amounts of international trade to be undertaken is the *trade indifference curve* (TI_0).

In a similar fashion we are now able to derive a whole set of trade indifference curves, each one corresponding to a different level of utility for the residents of the country. Each one of these trade indifference curves is generated by the same process of sliding the production possibility curve along a community indifference curve and letting the origin of the production possibility curve's coordinate system trace out the trade indifference curve. In Figure 5-3 we show a set of trade indifference curves generated in the manner described. One such curve, TI_1, was obtained by sliding the production possibility curve along the community indifference curve CIC_1.

A trade indifference curve shows all export-import combinations which

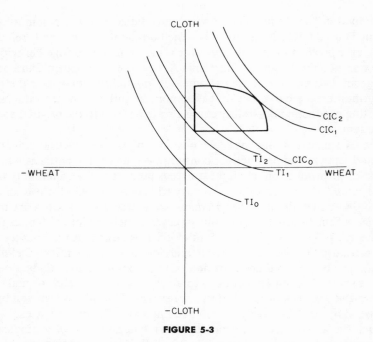

FIGURE 5-3

given a production possibility curve, will allow the country to reach a certain community indifference curve, thus permitting her to maintain a constant level of utility.

b. Slope of the Trade Indifference Curve

A direct relationship exists between the slope of the community indifference curve, the production possibility curve, and the trade indifference curve. These relationships are illustrated in Figure 5-4. Consider the shift of the production possibility curve from tangency position R to tangency position P. The origin of the production possibility curve moves from point T to point S, involving greater imports of e of cloth and greater exports of f of wheat. The consumption pattern will change from point R to point P, resulting in increased cloth consumption of b and decreased wheat consumption of a. At the same time, the production pattern is being rearranged. From production pattern R, measured with reference to origin T, we change to production pattern P with reference to origin S. To allow for better comparison, the location of production point P is also shown with reference to origin T. This point is labeled P′. The rearrangement of production patterns involves in this case a movement from point R to point P′ (measured in the same coordinate system), resulting in a decreased cloth production of c and an increased wheat production of d.

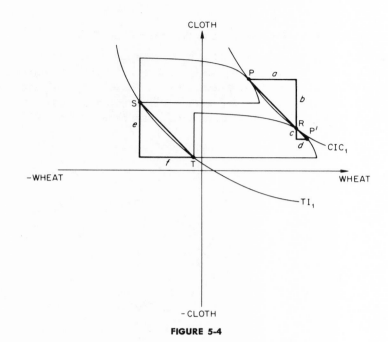

FIGURE 5-4

The total increase in cloth imports of e was therefore due to (1) an increase in cloth consumption by b, and (2) a decrease in cloth production of c. Also, the total increase in wheat exports of f was made possible by (1) a decrease of wheat consumption of a, and (2) an increase in wheat production of d. Therefore, it holds that:

$$b + c = e \quad \text{and} \quad a + d = f$$

A line between P and P′ would be parallel to ST. But PP′ is made up of the two segments PR and RP′. If we talk about very small, or infinitesimally small, shifts in the production possibility curve, we find that the slopes of the lines PR and RP′ tend to approximate the slope of the straight line PP′. Also, the slope of PR and RP′ will approximate the slope of the tangency at these points. For very small shifts of the production possibility curve we can therefore conclude that the slope of the community indifference curve is equal to the slope of the production possibility curve, which is also equal to the slope of the trade indifference curve.

At "corresponding" points on the community indifference curve, the production possibility curve, and the trade indifference curve, it holds that the marginal rate of substitution in consumption is equal to the marginal rate of transformation in production is equal to the marginal rate of export-import substitution.

c. From the Trade Indifference Curve to the Trade Offer Curve

In Section 4-2 we derived an offer curve showing the different quantities of commodities that a country wishes to trade, given various exchange ratios (terms of trade) between the two commodities. We will apply the same concept now to the problem of foreign trade, allowing for a rearrangement of consumption *and* production patterns at the same time.

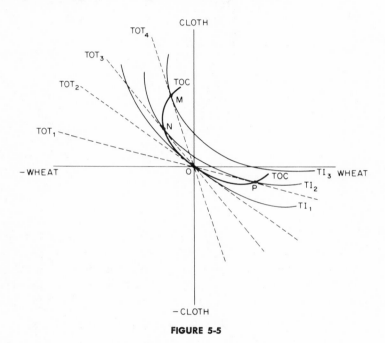

FIGURE 5-5

In Figure 5-5 we show a set of trade indifference curves and different terms of trade. Given the terms of trade TOT_2, the highest possible trade indifference curve which the country can reach is TI_1. The point of tangency is the origin O. Given the terms of trade TOT_3 and TOT_4, the country is able to attain tangency positions to TI_2 and TI_3 at points N and M respectively.

All the points of tangency of a trade indifference curve to a given terms of trade line show the optimal export-import pattern for the country. This optimal pattern will allow the country to reach the highest utility level consistent with her consumption and production patterns as well as with her trading opportunities. The collection of all points denoting the optimal trade pattern for each possible terms of trade is the international *trade offer curve*. The line through points M, N, O, and P shows such a trade offer curve (TOC).

Given any set of trade indifference curves, we are able to derive a trade offer curve by finding the trade patterns that will allow the country to attain the highest possible utility level under all possible terms of trade.

The trade offer curve is a helpful tool in international trade analysis because it allows us to tell at a glance the different commodity combinations a country is willing to trade at any given exchange ratio. For this reason we find the offer curve often referred to as a "willingness to trade curve." It also shows the total expenditures (i.e., exports in our case) of one commodity that a country is willing to make at any given exchange ratio in order to obtain a certain quantity of the other commodity (here, imports). From this function stems the name "total expenditure curve." Finally, the curve shows the demand for one commodity in terms of the other commodity, hence the name "reciprocal demand curve."

The usefulness and applicability of the tool to a wide variety of problems is foreshadowed by this long list of names, which directs our attention to the different purposes for which the trade offer curve can be used.

d. Elasticity of the Trade Offer Curve

In this section we will derive a geometric measure for the demand elasticity of the trade offer curve. Figure 5-6 shows the now familiar trade offer curve of a country, and indicates how many units of cloth will be imported (demanded) and how many of wheat will be exported (supplied) at different relative prices.

Let us assume that the price of cloth rises relative to wheat. This means that the terms of trade line rotates in a counterclockwise direction from TOT_1 to TOT_2. At the terms of trade TOT_1, the country wishes to import CO of cloth and is willing to export HO of wheat in exchange. At the new terms of trade TOT_2, the country will import GO and export JO.

We define now the price of elasticity of the offer curve as the percentage change in quantity over the percentage change in price. As long as we deal with discrete changes, we can write:

$$\text{El.} = \frac{\Delta Q/Q}{\Delta P/P} \tag{5-1}$$

Now we have to identify the relevant parameters in Figure 5-6. This is done in Table 5-1.

$$\text{El.} = \frac{\Delta Q/Q}{\Delta P/P} = \frac{CG/GO}{EF/FG} = \frac{HL/LO}{JL/LO} = \frac{HL}{JL} = \frac{DF}{EF} = \frac{HO}{KO} \tag{5-2}$$

A few words of explanation are in order. The measurement of the quantity of cloth demanded at the different terms of trade poses no problem. The percentage change in the quantity demanded due to the price change is CG/GO. The measurement of the price relationships is somewhat more com-

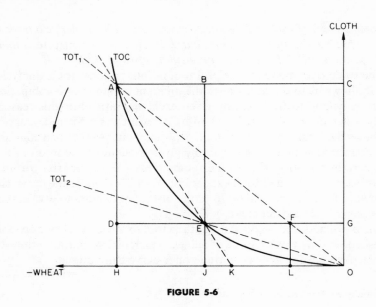

FIGURE 5-6

plicated. The slopes of the terms of trade lines indicate the relative price of cloth in terms of wheat: FG/GO at the terms of trade TOT$_1$ and EG/GO for TOT$_2$. If we take the distance GO as representing one unit of cloth, this simplifies to FG and EG respectively (see Table 5-1).

TABLE 5-1

	At TOT$_1$	At TOT$_2$	Change	Percentage Change
Quantity of Cloth	CO	GO	CG	$\dfrac{CG}{GO}$
Unit Price of Cloth in Terms of Wheat	FG	EG	EF	$\dfrac{EF}{FG}$

Once we have obtained the percentage changes of quantities and prices, we must reduce the information to some geometrically useful measure. First, we project all measures on the horizontal (wheat) axis. CG/GO becomes HL/LO because ACO and FGO are similar triangles, which results in equal relative size of their legs. EF/FG is simply projected on the horizontal axis, allowing us to rewrite it as JL/LO. The new expression for the elasticity simplifies now to HL/JL. Again we will use similar triangles to modify this geometric measure further. HL/JL can be rewritten as DF/EF. Then, because AFD and AOH are similar triangles, the distances DF/EF have to stay in the same relation as HO/KO.

Note that the point K is defined as the point at which a straight line through A and E cuts the horizontal axis. For very small or infinitesimally small changes in the terms of trade, the points A and E will tend to move closer and closer together. In this case the line through A and E will become the tangent to the offer curve. This gives us a ready measure for the elasticity of the offer curve at any given point. According to Equation 5-2, the elasticity of the offer curve is defined as HO/KO. This is the horizontal distance of the point on the offer curve at which the elasticity is to be evaluated, divided by the distance of the crossing point of a tangent to the offer curve and the horizontal axis.

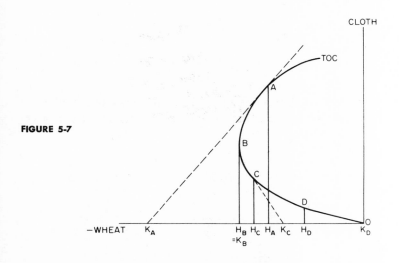

FIGURE 5-7

Figure 5-7 shows a trade offer curve. To derive the elasticity at any point, say, A, drop a perpendicular line to the horizontal axis and mark the intersection point H_A. Now draw a tangent to the trade offer curve at A. This tangent cuts the horizontal axis at K_A. The measure $H_A O/K_A O$ gives the elasticity of the trade offer curve at A. In this example the trade offer curve is clearly inelastic, as $H_A O$ is smaller than $K_A O$.

At point B the trade offer curve is unit elastic, as indicated by the equality of $H_B O$ and $K_B O$. At point C the curve is elastic (elasticity greater than one) as $H_C O$ is now greater than $K_C O$, resulting in an elasticity measure greater than one. Finally, at point D the offer curve is infinitely elastic. In the region between D and O, the offer curve is a straight line; thus the tangent at D is a straight line to the origin. The distance K_DO is equal to zero, and the elasticity H_DO/K_DO becomes infinity.

The simple geometric device of drawing a tangent and dropping a line perpendicular to the horizontal axis allows us to evaluate the elasticity of a trade offer curve. The elasticity of the offer curve will become important in connection with the stability conditions of equilibria for the terms of trade.

Also, for the country under consideration the elasticity of its trade offer curve is of great importance. It shows the policy makers how exports and imports will behave if the country is faced with a change in the terms of trade. The desired export performance is especially important in this context. If the offer curve is elastic, this means that additional imports will have to be paid for by a greater quantity of exports. If, however, the country should have an inelastic offer curve, changes in the terms of trade will allow the country to import a *larger* quantity of cloth in exchange for an absolutely *smaller* quantity of wheat exports.

3. The Terms of Trade

a. Equilibrium Terms of Trade

We have shown the quantities of the two commodities which one country is willing to trade as the collection of all points on the trade offer curve. To show which particular set of terms of trade will lead to equilibrium in inter-

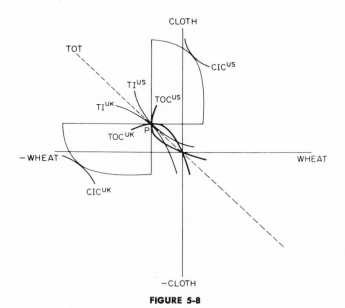

FIGURE 5-8

national markets, we have to introduce a second country, say, the United Kingdom.

In Figure 5-8 we draw the United Kingdom domestic indifference curve set in the lower left quadrant, exactly opposite the United States domestic indifference curve set, which lies as usual in the upper right quadrant. Utilizing the same technique we developed for the derivation of the United States trade indifference curves, we derive now the United Kingdom trade indifference curves. After drawing in the offer curves for both countries, TOC^{US} for the United States and TOC^{UK} for the United Kingdom, we are able to derive point P as the point of intersection of the trade offer curves for the two countries. At point P we will have an international trade equilibrium. The following conditions are fulfilled at this point: (1) we have one common exchange ratio of the two commodities as indicated by the terms of trade line TOT; (2) both countries have attained the highest possible trade indifference curve consistent with these terms of trade; and (3) the cloth imports by the United States are exactly equal to the exports of the same commodity by the United Kingdom, while the wheat exports by the United States are equal to the imports of the same commodity by the United Kingdom. Any other set of relative prices would result in different terms of trade, and at these different terms of trade one country would prefer to export more of a commodity than the other country would want to import, and vice versa. Such a situation could not provide an equilibrium solution. There would be forces in existence which would tend to return the terms of trade lines to their equilibrium position.

b. Demand Reversals and the Direction of Trade

It was pointed out above that the direction of trade is determined by the interaction of both supply and demand conditions. A change in demand patterns alone could be responsible for a change in the direction of trade.

These observations are of especially great importance in connection with the theory of comparative costs and the Heckscher-Ohlin theory of the structure of trade. Both of these theories focus attention on supply conditions alone as a determinant of international trade, and assume identical taste patterns. A *demand reversal* is defined as a condition where the commodity that a country is expected to export according to the theory of comparative costs or the Heckscher-Ohlin theory is actually imported because it is so highly demanded at home that the country will supplement its domestic production.

It may be true, for instance, that cloth is so highly demanded in the United Kingdom that, despite a comparative cost advantage in its production, the price will be driven up to a level higher than in the United States. As a consequence, the United Kingdom will tend to import cloth from the United States. This pattern of trade is a reversal of the one which would be predicted by taking cost considerations alone into account.

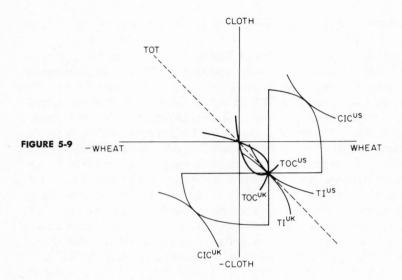

FIGURE 5-9

A demand reversal situation is shown in Figure 5-9, where the United States exports cloth at the equilibrium terms of trade TOT, while the United Kingdom exports wheat.

Finally, the possibility exists that the forces of supply and demand in each of the two countries balance each other in such a fashion that the same relative prices prevail. The slopes of the production possibility curves and the indifference curves are identical, and as a consequence the slope of the

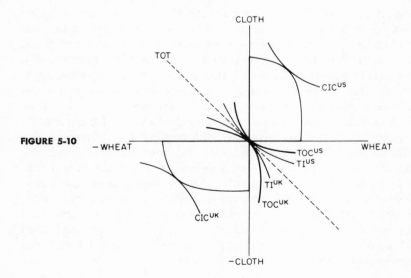

FIGURE 5-10

trade indifference curves are also the same in the no-trade situation. As all prices are already equalized, there is no reason for the emergence of international trade. Such a situation is shown in Figure 5-10.

Countries with widely different production possibility curves and indifference curve patterns will not trade with each other if the relative price ratios of the different commodities in the countries in isolation are identical.

Note that in all three cases, as shown in Figures 5-8, 5-9, and 5-10, the terms of trade are identical, as are the production possibility curves of the two countries. The only variable which is changed is the pattern of demand. As it changes, so does the direction of trade, as outlined above.

c. Multiple Equilibria and Stability Conditions

(i) *Multiple Equilibria*

It is possible that several different terms of trade exist that are consistent with equilibrium. One such situation is illustrated in Figure 5-11, where we

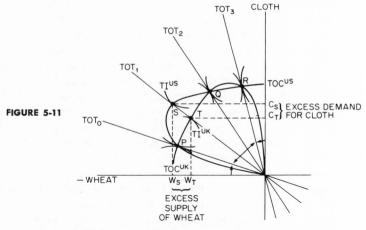

FIGURE 5-11

show the offer curves TOC^{US} and TOC^{UK}, representing the United States' and the United Kingdom's willingness to trade. A few of the international trade indifference curves belonging to each country are also shown. It will be noted that there are three points at which the two offer curves intersect. These points are labeled P, Q, and R. The volume of exports will be equal to the volume of imports at any one of these three points; we also find at each point two trade indifference curves which are tangent to each other.

(ii) *Stability Conditions*

There is nevertheless a substantial difference in the *type* of equilibrium which prevails at points P and R on the one hand and point Q on the other. To show the difference in the types of equilibrium, it will be useful to investigate what will happen if there is the slightest disturbance to the equilibrium situation. If there is a tendency for the same equilibrium to be restored after a disturbance, we will refer to this type of equilibrium as *stable*. If, however, a slight disturbance of the equilibrium will set up forces which will lead us even further away from equilibrium, we shall classify this situation as an *unstable equilibrium*.

Consider the terms of trade TOT_1, shown in Figure 5-11. The terms of trade TOT_1 could represent a disturbance of the initial equilibrium terms TOT_2. Let us investigate now whether there would be a tendency of the terms of trade to return to their initial TOT_2 position. In the situation shown in the figure, the United States exports wheat while it imports cloth. The opposite applies in the United Kingdom. At the terms of trade TOT_1, the United States will find a trade indifference curve tangent to the terms of trade line at point S. She will therefore be willing to export W_SO of wheat and to import C_SO of cloth. Similarly, the United Kingdom will find one of its trade indifference curves tangent to the terms of trade line at point T, making it want to export C_TO of cloth and to import W_TO of wheat. From the graph it is apparent that the quantity of wheat exports by the United States is greater than the quantity of wheat imports by the United Kingdom. Also, the quantity of cloth exports by the United Kingdom is smaller than the quantity of cloth imports by the United States. There will be an excess supply of wheat, and an excess demand for cloth. As a consequence, the price of wheat will tend to fall, while the price of cloth will tend to rise. Wheat will become cheaper in terms of cloth, which finds its expression in a counterclockwise rotation of the terms of trade line. Thus the terms of trade line TOT_1 will move *away* from the original terms of trade TOT_2. As there is no tendency for the equilibrium at point Q to be restored, we can conclude that point Q represents an unstable equilibrium.

We have shown that the terms of trade TOT_1 will be inclined to rotate counterclockwise. The process will come to a stop when the new equilibrium terms of trade TOT_0 are reached. At these terms of trade it will once again be true that the equilibrium conditions are fulfilled (point P). There will be no tendency for the terms of trade to move beyond TOT_0. If they should, forces will be set in action which will tend to push the terms of trade back to their equilibrium at TOT_0. Thus point P represents a stable equilibrium.

A similar argument applies to the equilibrium point R. It is also true here that if the equilibrium terms of trade are disturbed, there will be a tendency for the terms of trade to return to their original position and the equilibrium at point R to be restored.

We can conclude that points P and R are stable equilibria, and that Q is unstable. A stable equilibrium is characterized geometrically by the two countries' trade offer curves cutting each other from below (or from the inside, viewed from the origin). Unstable equilibria have trade offer curves cutting each other from above (or the outside). In general, it will be true that every unstable equilibrium point is surrounded by two stable equilibrium points. This case becomes important if there are a large number of intersections between the trade offer curves.

We are able to derive some more formal criteria for stability of equilibrium. Consider Figure 5-12. The trade offer curves are drawn so that they

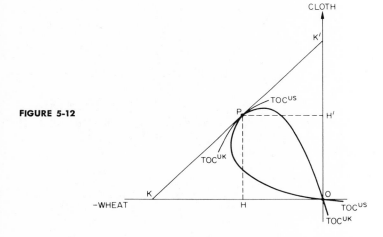

FIGURE 5-12

have the same slope at the point of equilibrium, point P. The elasticity measures derived in Section 5-2-d allow us to calculate the elasticities of the offer curves. The trade offer curve of the United States has the elasticity HO/KO at point P, while the United Kingdom's has the elasticity H'O/K'O. The United Kingdom's elasticity measure can be transformed as follows by considering similar triangles:

$$\frac{H'O}{K'O} = \frac{PH}{K'O} = \frac{KH}{KO} \tag{5-3}$$

The sum of the elasticities of the two countries together is

$$\frac{HO}{KO} + \frac{KH}{KO} = 1 \tag{5-4}$$

If the slopes of the trade offer curves at the point of equilibrium are identical, the sum of the elasticities will be equal to one.

Remembering that if the trade offer curves cut each other from the inside we will have a stable equilibrium, we can conclude that if the sum of the elasticities of the trade offer curves at the equilibrium point is larger than one, we have a stable equilibrium. Such a situation is shown in Figure 5-13, where the trade offer curves TOC^{US} and TOC$_2^{UK}$ cut each other from below. Conversely, if the sum of the elasticities of the trade offer curves is smaller than one, we

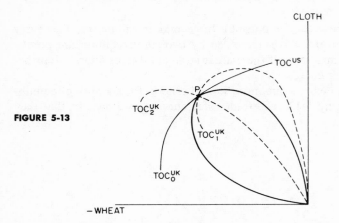

FIGURE 5-13

have an unstable equilibrium. Trade offer curves TOC^{US} and TOC_1^{UK} may serve as an illustration. The borderline case of elasticities summing to one, which served as the starting point of this analysis, will occupy our attention somewhat more in the following section.

(iii) Regions of Indeterminacy

Finally, the possibility arises that the trade offer curves of the two countries may overlap in a region. This case is shown in Figure 5-14. The offer

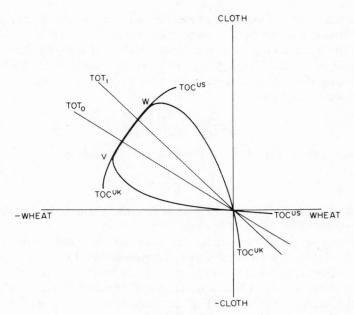

FIGURE 5-14

curves of the United States and the United Kingdom have the same slope and therefore coincide in the region between points V and W. The elasticities will sum to one. *Any* terms of trade line which crosses the trade offer curves between these two points will represent a stable set of prices. A movement away from an original terms of trade line, such as TOT_0 to TOT_1, will not set in motion any forces which would tend either to turn the terms of trade line even further or to return it to the original position. Thus we have a region of indeterminacy, within which we cannot decide how the terms of trade will adjust themselves. International exchange may take place at any one of an infinite number of terms of trade.

(iv) *Relevance to Policy Decisions*

The question of multiple equilibria and stability of these equilibria is of great importance in policy decisions of individual countries. Consider the position of the United States in the multiple equilibria case discussed in Section (i) above and illustrated by Figure 5-11. If the United States faces the terms of trade TOT_0, she will export and import a commodity combination depicted by point P. Slight disturbances of equilibrium will lead to a re-establishment of the stable equilibrium terms of trade TOT_0. A study of the situation will reveal that point P is optimal in the sense that all conditions for the best possible allocation of resources are fulfilled.

However, there exists the stable equilibrium point R, which can be reached if the terms of trade change drastically. A big push is needed to change the terms of trade beyond the point at which they would return to the original equilibrium position at P. If the country succeeds in pushing the terms of trade beyond TOT_2, they will be moved on to TOT_3 by market forces. Once the position R has been reached, the United States could import a much *larger* quantity of cloth for a *smaller* quantity of wheat exports than before.

For the policy maker it is therefore important not to focus attention solely on the fulfillment of the optimum *marginal* conditions, but to look out also for the *total* conditions of the situation at hand. Only a knowledge of the full trade offer will permit the policy maker to render a judgment.

Similarly, if the country should be faced with the terms of trade TOT_2, which were identified as being unstable equilibrium terms of trade in our example, any attempt to maintain these terms of trade is doomed to fail. The slightest disturbance in international markets will move the equilibrium terms of trade all the way to P or R. If the policy makers realize early enough that the situation they face is an unstable one, they might take action which would make it possible to reach the more favorable of the stable terms of trade which surround the unstable equilibrium.

Finally, if the country should find herself in a zone of indeterminacy, as depicted in Figure 5-14, it would be possible to move the terms of trade at will to any position within the zone. Naturally, the country would want to take the opportunity to influence the terms of trade in order to import the greatest quantity of commodities in exchange for exporting the smallest possible quantity. Only if the country actually realizes that it is operating in such a zone of indeterminacy will it be able to take full advantage of the situation. Otherwise the country might assume that the terms of trade are in a stable equilibrium position and fail to take any action.

4. The Constant Cost Case

In the previous analysis we assumed throughout that the country experiences increasing opportunity cost in the production of both commodities. In the case of constant opportunity costs of production, we are able to observe some interesting phenomena which will lead to important policy conclusions concerning the effect of country size on international trade. Some of the results to be derived have already been foreshadowed in Section 2-4.

a. Constant Cost Offer Curve

In the upper right quadrant of Figure 5-15 we show the familiar domestic community indifference curve CIC_0 and the production possibility block NMO, exhibiting constant opportunity costs. When we start to slide the pro-

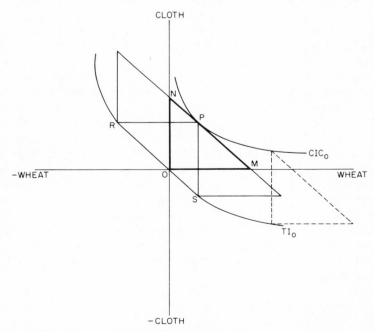

FIGURE 5-15

duction possibility curve along the indifference curve in order to generate the international trade indifference curve, we observe that the point of tangency (P) does not immediately change its position on the indifference curve. As a result, we find that the trade indifference curve will be a straight line in the segment RS, which lies parallel to the line NM. Only after the production possibility curve touches the indifference curve with one of its endpoints (N or M) will the international trade indifference curve assume the familiar curvature.

As soon as either one of the endpoints of the production possibility curve touches the indifference curve, the country is completely specialized. No further increase of production of one commodity is possible, and the trade indifference curve will run parallel to the community indifference curve, where the displacement is given by the size of the production possibility curve.

Given a set of trade indifference curves, such as shown in Figure 5-16, we are able to derive the country's trade offer curve. This is done by the familiar method of taking the points of tangency of different trade indifference curves to all possible terms of trade lines. In the region OA, the terms of trade line TOT_0 coincides with the slope of the trade indifference curve TI_0. The

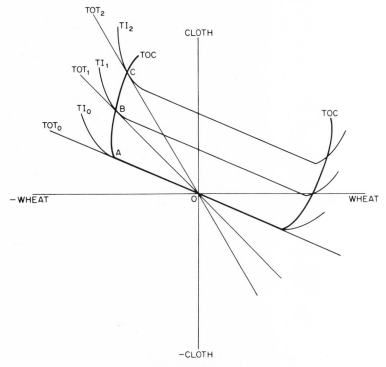

FIGURE 5-16

trade indifference curve is therefore identical to the trade offer curve in the OA segment. Given the terms of trade TOT_1, tangency will occur at point B, while the terms of trade TOT_2 allow for tangency at point C. The line connecting OABC is the trade offer curve for the constant cost case.

The trade offer curve of a country which experiences constant cost in production is characterized by a linear segment.

b. Effects of Country Size on Trade and Specialization

We can make some interesting observations on the patterns of international trade and specialization that evolve as a consequence of size differences between countries. We will use the constant cost case to illustrate the principles involved, although similar patterns of complete and incomplete specialization can also be found in the increasing and decreasing cost cases. In constant cost situations we find the analysis particularly straightforward and unambiguous.

(i) Countries of Equal Size

In Figure 5-17 we show the trade offer curves for the United States and the United Kingdom, which are assumed to be of roughly equal size. The trade offer curves intersect at point E, which defines the equilibrium terms of

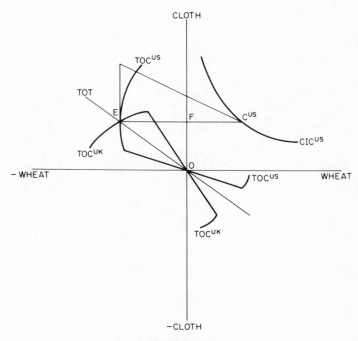

FIGURE 5-17

trade and the quantities which each country wishes to export and import at this international exchange ratio. Point E is located in the curved section of the offer curves of the two countries, indicating that both countries are completely specialized in production.

Let us focus attention on the United States case. The United States wishes to import OF of cloth in exchange for EF of wheat exports. She wants to do this in order to be able to attain consumption point C^{US}, which is located on the highest community indifference curve that can be reached (CIC^{US}). The country's production possibility curve touches the community indifference curve with one of its endpoints at C^{US}. The country specializes completely, producing EC^{US} of wheat. Only FC^{US} of the total wheat production is consumed at home, leaving EF for export purposes.

It will be noted that the pretrade United States exchange ratio coincides with the slope of the production possibility curve. The same is true of the United Kingdom. Demand patterns of the two countries are influential in determining the precise position of the terms of trade line between the limits set by the pretrade domestic exchange ratios.

We can conclude that under constant cost conditions countries of equal size will tend to specialize completely in the production of the commodity in which they have a comparative advantage.

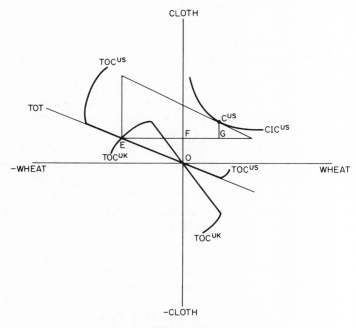

FIGURE 5-18

(ii) Countries of Unequal Size

In Figure 5-18 we show the trade offer curves of a large country, say, the United States, and a small country, say, the United Kingdom. If the two countries' offer curves intersect in the straight segment of the larger country's offer curve, the small country will specialize completely, while the large country will continue to produce both commodities. In our example the United Kingdom's trade offer curve intersects the United States' offer curve at E. The United States will produce EG of wheat and $C^{US}G$ of cloth. She will export EF of her total wheat production in exchange for FO of cloth, allowing her to consume a commodity bundle depicted by point C^{US}.

Note that the international terms of trade coincide with the domestic terms of trade of the large country. This is because production takes place under constant cost conditions and because the large country continues to produce both commodities. As the large country is presumably able to produce additional wheat or cloth under the same cost conditions under which she is actually producing, any changes will not disturb the exchange ratio prevailing in the market.

If countries are of unequal size, the smaller one will specialize completely, while the larger one may continue to produce both commodities. The international terms of trade will coincide with the pretrade domestic exchange ratio of the larger country if specialization is incomplete.

5. Multi-Country and Multi-Commodity Cases

Up to now we have limited ourselves to the two-country, two-commodity case. In this section we will extend the analysis to cover any arbitrary number of countries and in the following section we will analyze the many-commodity case.

In Section 5-2-c we derived the international trade offer curve for a country. We will recall that the offer curve shows the quantities of the commodities which the country in question is willing to trade at any given set of terms of trade. If we want to extend our analysis to include more than two countries and commodities, we must devise a technique which will allow us to aggregate the two-country, two-commodity offer curves.

a. Many Countries

Let us turn first to the case of many countries and two commodities. Each country will have a trade offer curve derived in the fashion described above. In Figure 5-19 we show the offer curves for the United States (TOC^{US}) and the United Kingdom (TOC^{UK}). At the terms of trade TOT$_1$ the United Kingdom does not want to import cloth in exchange for wheat. The United States,

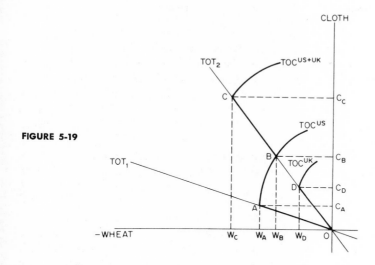

FIGURE 5-19

however, is willing to import OC_A of cloth in exchange for OW_A of wheat. Since the United Kingdom does not want to import cloth and export wheat at these terms of trade, the offer curve for the two countries combined coincides with the offer curve of the United States.

As the terms of trade change, say, to TOT_2, the United Kingdom will enter the market. At the new terms of trade she will be willing to import OC_D of cloth in exchange for OW_D of wheat. The United States wants to trade OC_B of cloth for OW_B of wheat. If we sum the quantities that each country wants to trade individually, we get the aggregate amounts that the two countries together are willing to trade. At the terms of trade TOT_2 the two countries together want to import OC_C of cloth in exchange for OW_C of wheat, where OC_B plus OC_D is equal to OC_C, and OW_B plus OW_D equals OW_C. Thus a new point C is defined, which represents OC_C of cloth imports and OW_C of wheat exports. This point C shows the quantities that the two countries together are willing to trade and is therefore one point on the combined trade offer curve for the United Kingdom and the United States. By rotating the terms of trade line slowly and observing the new combined quantities of trade, we are able to generate a new trade offer curve for the two countries together. Such a trade offer curve for the United Kingdom and the United States is shown in the figure by the line OABC, and is labeled TOC^{US+UK}.

In principle it is possible to add the trade offer curves for any number of countries by the method described and to arrive at a trade offer curve for the world as a whole. Note that as the terms of trade change, making cloth a cheaper commodity as indicated by a rotation of the terms of trade line from TOT_1 to TOT_2, more countries will want to import cloth and export wheat.

By aggregating the trade offer curves for all countries we are able to derive a world trade offer curve for the two commodities. There are some countries that wish to import wheat in exchange for cloth. These countries will generate an aggregate trade offer curve which crosses the trade offer curve of the cloth-importing countries. The intersection will determine the world terms of trade between cloth and wheat. As long as there are any countries that have excess demands or excess supplies at the world terms of trade, the terms of trade will continue to adjust until all such excess demands and supplies are eliminated.

To find the amounts which individual countries will want to trade once the world terms of trade are set, we have to go back to the individual trade offer curves and check the amounts which the country wants to export and import at the exchange rate set in the world market.

If we aggregate the trade offer curves of several countries which are characterized by constant cost conditions, we will find that the aggregate trade offer curves for the country groups will have several linear segments. Each linear segment coincides with the domestic terms of trade of a country. If the intersection of two aggregate trade offer curves falls within one of these linear segments, the country whose domestic cost ratio coincides with the international terms of trade may not specialize completely.

Three cases are possible: (1) The aggregate trade offer curves may intersect in a linear segment of each one of the trade offer curves. Such a situation is shown in Figure 5-20a. The international terms of trade coincide with the

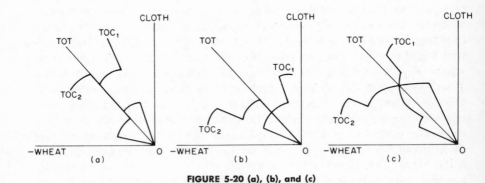

FIGURE 5-20 (a), (b), and (c)

domestic terms of trade of *two* countries: the second country represented on trade offer curve TOC_1 and also the second country represented on trade offer curve TOC_2. Slight changes in demand patterns are not likely to influence the terms of trade at all, as there is a considerable region of overlap of the two aggregate trade offer curves. Any shift which does not move the point of intersection out of this region of overlap is not going to change the terms of trade at all. (2) If the aggregate trade offer curves intersect as shown in Figure 5-20b, we have a situation in which the country on trade offer curve TOC_1 is specialized completely, while the country on trade offer curve TOC_2 continues to produce both commodities. The situation here is very similar to the one described in Section 5-4-b-ii, where we dealt with the effects of country size on specialization and trade patterns. Again, small shifts in demand patterns are not likely to alter the terms of trade. Finally, (3) we have the possibility that the two aggregate trade offer curves intersect in one of the curved sections of the aggregate trade offer curve. Under these circumstances all countries will be completely specialized, and the terms of trade are sensitive to small demand shifts.

We should note here that as the number of countries increases greatly, the relative size of the linear segments of the aggregate trade offer curves becomes smaller and smaller. The pessimism that demand conditions are not important as far as the determination of the terms of trade is concerned is therefore unfounded. Only if we have a world made up of very few countries, all operating under constant cost conditions, are we likely to find that small demand shifts do not influence the terms of trade at all.

The aggregate trade offer curves of a group of countries which experience constant costs in production are characterized by linear segments. As the number of countries increases, the linear segments will become relatively smaller, and the aggregate trade offer curve will resemble a smooth curve.

Naturally, under conditions of increasing costs the linear segments will not be found at all. The aggregate trade offer curve may, however, be characterized by kinks at the terms of trade at which a new country enters the market. Otherwise the derivation of the aggregate trade offer curve under increasing cost conditions parallels the one under constant cost conditions.

b. Many Commodities

Under constant cost conditions it is also possible to extend the analysis to the many-commodity case. For simplicity's sake we will assume that there are only two countries, each with resources that can be grouped into homogeneous "bales," which are in turn able to produce certain commodities in a fixed ratio. Thus one bale might be used to produce x units of cloth, y units of wheat, or z units of pizza. After we have decided how many bales of resources are to be devoted to the production of each commodity, we can draw up a trade offer curve for the different commodities which can be produced with the bales at hand. The cost of the commodity in terms of bales of resources is shown by the slope of the trade offer curve. The number of linear segments of the trade offer curve coincides with the number of commodities under consideration. The country will be the sole producer of all commodities which lie below the point of intersection on the aggregate trade offer curve and will *not* produce any commodities which lie above it. The country will share in the production of any commodities whose linear segment happens to lie at the crossing point of the two trade offer curves. Conditions for complete or incomplete specialization in commodities are identical to the ones discussed for different countries in the preceding section. All we have to do is replace the word "country" with "commodity."

6. Empirical Evidence

A theory as general as the one outlined in this chapter is not very useful for policy purposes. Economic policy is concerned with the economic effects of a change in the parameters which can be influenced by governmental authorities. The theory presented here predicts that, essentially, anything can happen. A change in any one parameter can always be offset by a change in the opposite direction of another parameter.

For this reason it is difficult to test the theory empirically. Few, if any, testable empirical propositions could be derived which could be either rejected or validated by the data available.

The usefulness of the general equilibrium model lies, therefore, not so much in its ability to generate empirically useful predictions, but in the help it provides in understanding the interaction of the variables of the economic system. Only if one has a firm grasp of the interdependency of the different variables is one able to take account of a whole multitude of possible reactions.

The two most popular theories of the structure of trade, the comparative cost theory and the simple Heckscher-Ohlin theory, restrict themselves to the supply side only, assuming no international differences in tastes. One of the outstanding characteristics of the general equilibrium trade model which grew out of the simple Heckscher-Ohlin model is that it takes into account demand and supply patterns at the same time.

From all the empirical evidence available on consumption patterns we concluded (see Section 4-3) that demand is an important factor in determining the structure of international trade between countries with widely different per capita income levels. It was pointed out in this chapter that there exists the possibility of demand reversals, which would invalidate the predictions of the Heckscher-Ohlin theory.

Some of the disappointing results of the empirical verification of the Heckscher-Ohlin model (see Section 3-2-d) may be explained by the existence of these demand reversals. As the likelihood of demand reversals increases with increasing disparity in the per capita income levels between countries, we should expect that countries with widely different per capita income levels will be affected by demand reversals. These conditions are fulfilled for two of the three cases in which the simple Heckscher-Ohlin theory yielded unsatis-factory predictions. The large income differential between the United States and the rest of the world, as well as the more specific instance of India and the United States are cases in point. These two cases involve probably the largest per capita income differentials of any of the studies, and the chance for a demand reversal is therefore great.

Note that we are not able to state definitely that it is demand reversals which are actually responsible for the perverse predictions, since there is no evidence to compel us to exclude other factors which might have influenced the empirical results actually obtained. Nevertheless, these findings are im-portant because they present evidence that foreign trade cannot be explained in terms of supply conditions alone, and show that demand may be just as important a factor influencing the pattern of world trade.

It is here that the basic framework of the Heckscher-Ohlin model does valuable service in that it pinpoints many of the crucial variables which are relevant to the problem of determining the direction and composition of trade. Many questions of methodology, especially as far as the usefulness of economic theory is concerned, are treated at greater length in Chapter 1.

SUGGESTED FURTHER READINGS

Becker, Gary, "A Note on Multi-Country Trade," *American Economic Review*, September 1952.

Elliott, George, "The Theory of International Values," *Journal of Political Economy*, February 1950.

Graham, Frank, "The Theory of International Values Reexamined," *Quarterly Journal of Economics*, November 1923 (reprinted in H. Ellis and L. Metzler, *Readings in the Theory of International Trade*. Homewood, Ill.: Richard D. Irwin, 1949, Chapter 14).

Kleiman, E., "Comparative Advantage, Graham's Theory, and Activity Analysis," *Economica*, August 1960.

Meade, James, *A Geometry of International Trade*. London: Allen & Unwin, 1952, Chapters 1–4.

Metzler, Lloyd, "Graham's Theory of International Values," *American Economic Review*, June 1950.

Vanek, Jaroslav, *International Trade: Theory and Economic Policy*. Homewood, Ill.: Richard D. Irwin, 1962, Chapter 14.

Whitin, Thomas, "Classical Theory, Graham's Theory, and Linear Programming in International Trade," *Quarterly Journal of Economics*, November 1953.

CHAPTER 6

Effects of International Trade on the Factors of Production

In Chapters 3 and 5 we had occasion to refer to the interrelationships between factors of production and the production possibilities of a country. But we refrained from making any specific statements about the effects of international trade on factor prices and factor quantities supplied. The present chapter will analyze these effects.

1. Definition of a Factor of Production

The definitions of a factor of production, factor abundance, factor scarcity, and comparative cheapness of a factor are important. Much confusion about the effects of international trade on factor prices and factor supplies stems from the fact that people associate different concepts with the same words.

Often the definition of a factor of production is not entirely unambiguous. We will classify as one factor of production all resources composed of individual units which can be exchanged against each other in any production process without resulting in a change in the output level. In other words, only resources which are perfect substitutes for each other will be classified under the same factor of production heading.

It is clear that the time element plays a crucial role in the definition of a factor of production. In the short run most capital is embodied in its present use in the sense that it cannot be shifted into another use. Capital equipment is characterized by the fact that it tends to wear out in use. Once a piece of capital equipment is fully physically depreciated, it has to be replaced by a new piece of equipment. At this time we have the choice of building a different piece of capital equipment. In the long run then we have a choice between one piece of capital equipment and another. The crucial observation to be made is that in the long run capital is more homogeneous than in the short run. In the long run capital can be shifted between different production processes without affecting the output level, while this is not possible in the short run when much of the capital is embodied.

Similar considerations apply to the other factor of production: labor. Workers have to be retrained before they can be employed in different production processes, and often the retraining process is very costly. Again, in the long run these shifts are easier. New entrants into the labor force can choose between different occupations, and they are very mobile before they have started their training process. Once the training process has started, it is more difficult to change over to a different occupation.

The other concepts which need careful definition are: abundance, scarcity, and relative cheapness of a factor. We will use the words abundance and scarcity only when we are talking about physical factor endowments. The words cheapness and expensiveness will be referred to in connection with values of factors of production. Physical measures of amounts of factors of production take account of supply conditions of the factors only; value measures reflect the interaction of supply and demand. Quite often we will find that physical abundance and cheapness coincide. But there are cases where demand for the physically abundant factor is so high that it actually becomes the relatively expensive factor in value terms. Because it is difficult to compare physical abundance of different factors of production in the absence of a common measuring rod, we will always talk about the relative abundance of capital and labor in one country as opposed to another country. In other words, we will be primarily interested in comparing capital/labor ratios in different countries.

2. Factor Price Changes Caused by Trade

a. Direction of Factor Price Changes

Figure 6-1 depicts a production possibility curve and an Edgeworth Box showing isoquants for the two commodities cloth and wheat.[1] We will assume that the country shown in the diagram is relatively (to the other country) labor abundant and capital scarce. Also, the usual catalogue of assumptions is assumed to hold true.

In isolation the country will produce at point A (Figure 6-1a), where her

---

[1] These basic concepts are reviewed in the Appendix.

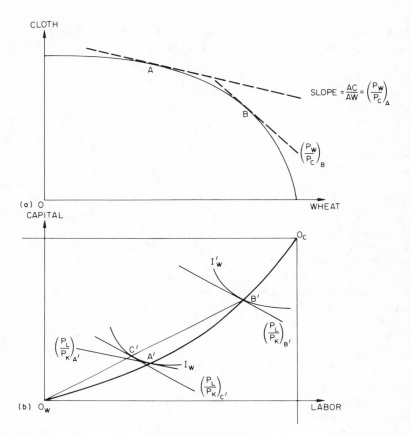

FIGURE 6-1 (a) and (b)

production possibility curve is tangent to a community indifference curve (not shown in the diagram). The relative price ratio of wheat to cloth is given by the slope of the common tangency at point A. The optimal factor utilization pattern associated with the production pattern A is given by point A′ in Figure 6-1b. Point A′ is a point on the contract curve, characterized by the tangency of a wheat isoquant to a cloth isoquant (not shown in the diagram). The slope of the common tangency to the two isoquants at point A′ shows the ratio at which capital can be substituted for labor, and is equal to the relative price ratio of labor to capital.

As soon as international trade starts, the country will tend to export the commodity (wheat) which is relatively intensive in her relatively abundant factor (labor). Trade will increase the relative price of the commodity (wheat) which the country exports. This is shown in Figure 6-1a by the movement from A to B, resulting in a steeper price line, which indicates that wheat has become more expensive in terms of cloth.

As wheat production expands, resources have to be taken out of cloth production and transferred to wheat production. But the factors are not released in the contracting cloth industry in the same proportion as they are needed in wheat production. As a consequence, the price of the factor which is used intensively in the expanding wheat industry, namely, labor, will be driven up relatively to the price of capital. In Figure 6-1b resource use patterns change from point A' (before trade) to B' (after trade). The tangent to the isoquants at point B', $\left(\dfrac{P_L}{P_K}\right)_B$, is steeper than the tangent to the isoquants at A', $\left(\dfrac{P_L}{P_K}\right)_A$, indicating that the price of labor has increased relatively to the price of capital.

The relative steepness of the tangents (factor price lines) at A' and B' follows immediately from the homogeneity assumption which underlies our model. Homogeneous isoquants have equal slopes along any ray from the origin. The slopes of the two wheat isoquants shown are the same at points B' and C'. As point A' is located on the same isoquant, to the right of point C', and as isoquants are convex to the origin, the slope of the isoquant must be flatter at point A' than at C'. And as the slope at C' is equal to the slope at B', the slope at A' must be flatter than at B'. The steeper slope of the factor price line at B' indicates that the P_L/P_K ratio has increased, which means that the price of labor has increased relatively to the price of capital.

It is possible to condense much of the information contained in Figures 6-1a and 6-1b into one diagram. This is done in Figure 6-2. Later this translation will allow us to derive more readily the conditions for complete factor price equalization in different countries.

Along the vertical axis of Figure 6-2a we measure the slope of the *product* price line, which shows the price of wheat over the price of cloth, P_W/P_C. On the horizontal axis we measure the slope of the *factor* price line, showing the price of labor over the price of capital, P_L/P_K. In the diagram we plot the slopes of the corresponding product and factor price ratios of Figures 6-1a and 6-1b. The two points A'' and B'' show the price ratios corresponding to points A and B (product price ratio) and A' and B' (factor price ratio). By plotting all possible price ratios, we are able to generate the line RR', which shows the commodity-price factor-price relations prevailing in the country.

Each country has a certain physical capital/labor ratio, and, given the shape of the isoquants, only a limited range of labor/capital price ratios is possible. This general idea is conveyed in Figure 6-2b, where the physical capital/labor endowment ratio of the country (i.e., an expression for the size of the Edgeworth Box) is shown along the vertical axis, and the by now familiar labor/capital price ratio along the horizontal axis.

Given any labor/capital price ratio, we are able to find the physical capital/labor ratio which should be used in the production of each commodity.

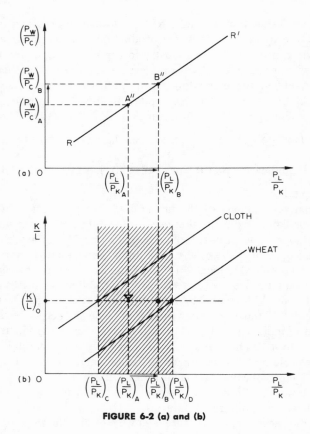

FIGURE 6-2 (a) and (b)

The optimal capital/labor ratios for different labor/capital price ratios are shown in Figure 6-2b for the commodities cloth and wheat. Note that the relatively capital-intensive commodity cloth uses a higher capital/labor ratio at each factor price ratio than does wheat. The line for cloth always lies above the line for wheat, indicating that cloth production is always more capital intensive than wheat production.

Individual countries must decide on an optimal pattern of production and specialization. If a country decides to trade internationally, she will have to rearrange her production patterns to adjust herself to the new situation. Two parameters are especially important in the country's decision: (1) her overall capital/labor endowment ratio, and (2) the world price ratio of the commodities she produces or is interested in trading.

For any given product price ratio P_W/P_C we have a unique factor price ratio P_L/P_K. These two variables are plotted in Figure 6-2a. In our example the two ratios always change in the same direction. If P_W/P_C rises, so does

P_L/P_K. This is due to the fact that an increase in the price of the factor of production (say, labor), which is used intensively in a product (wheat), will increase the price of this product more than the price of the other product (cloth). In the previous diagram (Figure 6-1b) this was indicated by an increasing slope of the factor price ratio. It will also be true that an increased product (say, wheat) price will attract new factors of production into the industry. But proportionately more of the factor of production (labor) which is intensive in the expanding industry is required. This increased labor can be hired only at higher wages, thus increasing the labor/capital factor price ratio. In Figure 6-1b this was indicated by an increasing slope of the factor price ratio P_L/P_K as we moved from point A' to point B'.

Figure 6-2b shows how much of a country's resources are devoted to the production of each one of the two commodities. The overall capital/labor ratio for a country is given and is labeled $(K/L)_0$.

If the factor price ratio were equal to or any lower than $(P_L/P_K)_C$, the country would find it advantageous to produce only cloth, while at any factor price ratio greater than or equal to $(P_L/P_K)_D$ the country would specialize completely in wheat production. Factor prices are free to change between the limits set by $(P_L/P_K)_C$ and $(P_L/P_K)_D$. We might want to call this zone the *feasible region* for factor price changes.

After the country enters into international trade the product price ratio will change from $(P_W/P_C)_A$ to $(P_W/P_C)_B$, the international terms of trade. As there is a direct relationship between the product price ratio and the factor price ratio, the prices of factors of production will adjust to take account of the product price change. In Figure 6-2a we will move from point A'' to B'', which implies a move in the factor price ratio from $(P_L/P_K)_A$ to $(P_L/P_K)_B$. The factor price change is accompanied by a shift in the production pattern from cloth to wheat production. This result conforms to the one obtained from Figures 6-1a and 6-1b.

b. Factor Price Equalization

We will return to our two-country model to show the effects of international trade on the prices of the factors of production. We will be especially interested in the possibility of factor price equalization as a result of free international trade. Under certain assumptions it is possible to show that absolute factor prices will in fact be equalized if the countries engage in free international trade.

(i) The Factor Price Equalization Theorem

It is customary at this juncture to restate the whole list of assumptions necessary to assure factor price equalization in our model. The assumptions are:

1. Two countries;
2. Two commodities and two factors of production;
3. Perfect competition;
4. Linear homogeneous production functions;
5. Identical production functions in different countries;
6. Diminishing marginal productivity of factors;
7. Absence of complete specialization;
8. Absence of factor intensity reversals;
9. Perfectly inelastic factor supply curves for each country;
10. Absence of tariffs and transport costs.

In Section 6-3 below we will try to relax these assumptions and see which ones are necessary to validate the factor price equalization theorem.

Factor price equalization relies on the existence of several important links: for one, we must have completely free international trade, so that the prices of the traded products will be equated in all countries. Also, prices of

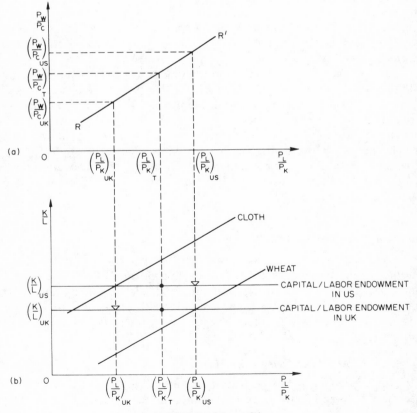

FIGURE 6-3 (a) and (b)

commodities must accurately reflect the cost of producing them. From this it follows that the marginal cost of producing a given traded commodity is the same in all countries. Finally, because production functions in the different countries are identical, the relationship between factor earnings and product cost is the same in all countries. The link between equal product prices and equal factor earnings is therefore established.

A word of caution may be in order: in the previous paragraph we asserted that the "marginal cost of production . . . is the same in all countries." Note that this statement refers to the production costs of the very last unit of each commodity which the country produces after trade has started. If additional units could be produced at a (relatively) lower cost than in the other country, the country would actually produce them and export them to the other countries. Differences in relative production costs are a precondition for the emergence of international trade, but the rise of international trade will eliminate any existing differences. Ex-ante factor prices (just like product prices) are different, while ex-post prices are identical.

The wheat/cloth price ratios that prevail in each country before trade are shown in Figure 6-3a as $(P_W/P_C)_{US}$ and $(P_W/P_C)_{UK}$. In Figure 6-3b we show the capital/labor endowment ratios $(K/L)_{US}$ and $(K/L)_{UK}$ for the United States and the United Kingdom respectively. These conditions imply a set of factor price ratios (shown along the horizontal axis of both figures) of $(P_L/P_K)_{US}$ and $(P_L/P_K)_{UK}$. Britain will tend to export her relatively cheap commodity, wheat, and the United States will tend to export cloth. International trade will equalize the product prices, and, since the product prices are related directly to the factor prices, these will be equalized, too. The final world product price ratio with trade is $(P_W/P_C)_T$, and the factor price ratio is $(P_L/P_K)_T$. Note that the physical capital/labor endowment ratios in the two countries do not change at all. The only variables free to adjust to the product price changes are the factor prices.

We can conclude that under certain assumptions international trade will lead to absolute factor price equalization.

It may be worth our while to note here that the changing factor prices imply that the income distribution within each country will change. Some factors of production will receive a higher remuneration, while others will experience a drop in their earnings. The consequences of the factor price changes for the income distribution will be spelled out in greater detail in Section 8-3.

(ii) Factor Demand Reversals and Factor Price Equalization

In the beginning of this chapter we pointed out that there is an important distinction between physical abundance of a factor of production and its cheapness. This distinction becomes important in the case of the so-called factor demand reversal.

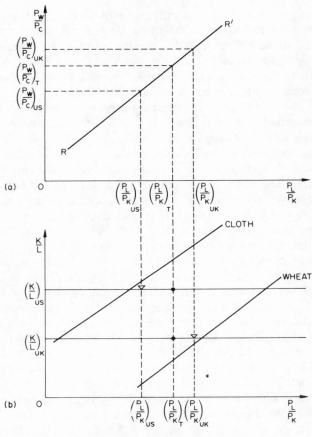

FIGURE 6-4 (a) and (b)

The expression demand reversal refers here to the phenomenon that the demand for a factor of production can be so strong that its relative price is higher in the country in which it is relatively abundant as far as physical endowment is concerned. This demand reversal occurs only if the commodity which is intensive in the physically abundant factor is in very great demand in the country under consideration.[2] The high demand for the product will lead to a high derived demand for the factor which is used intensively in production, thus raising the factor's price to a comparatively high level despite its relative abundance in physical terms.

Figure 6-4 illustrates such a case. The ratio (P_W/P_C) is higher in the United Kingdom than in the United States, the result of the great demand for wheat in Britain. Correspondingly, the ratio (P_L/P_K) is very high in the United

---

[2] See Section 5-3 for a fuller explanation of the simple demand reversal case.

Kingdom, too. The high value attached to labor stands in contrast to the relative physical abundance of labor which exists in Britain. Before trade the United Kingdom specializes almost completely in wheat, the commodity which is intensive in her physically *scarce* factor—capital. Similarly, the United States specializes in cloth, which is intensive in her scarce factor—land.

Free international trade will lead to product price equalization, which in turn will equalize factor prices. The important observation to be made is that the *direction* of trade is reversed: the United Kingdom imports wheat, the commodity which is intensive in her physically abundant factor—labor. However, labor is relatively expensive in value terms in Britain. The United States imports cloth, which is intensive in her physically abundant factor—capital, capital being the factor which is relatively expensive in value terms.

The pattern of international specialization is dictated not by physical abundance ratios, but by the criterion that a country tends to export (import) the commodity which is intensive in her relatively cheap (expensive) factor of production.

c. Obstacles to Factor Price Equalization

In this section we will scrutinize the assumptions underlying the factor price equalization theorem stated in the previous section. At the same time this section will serve to reassemble all the assumptions explicitly.

(i) Many Countries

There is no reason why we should not generalize the factor price equalization theorem to any number of countries. As long as the production functions are identical in all countries, and all the other assumptions are fulfilled, we will find that international trade will equalize commodity prices and thereby induce factor price equalization in all countries.

(ii) Many Products and Factors of Production

We are able to extend the factor price equalization theorem to the many-product, many-factor case, as long as for each factor price which has to be determined there is at least one product price to determine it. To put the matter the other way around: if the number of factors should exceed the number of products, then we do not have enough information contained in the product prices to allow us to determine all the factor prices. The system would be undetermined. But as long as the number of factors does not exceed the number of products, factor price equalization will be guaranteed.

(iii) Imperfect Competition

As soon as the assumption of perfect competition is dropped, the identity of marginal unit cost and product price is destroyed. Also, factors of production will no longer be paid the value of their marginal product. As the direct link between product prices and factor earnings is broken, we can no longer say that product price equalization will lead to factor price equalization. The assumption of perfect competition is a necessary one which cannot be relaxed.

(iv) Increasing Returns to Scale

As soon as there are increasing returns to scale in the production of one commodity, perfect competition will break down. We have shown already in Section (iii) that the assumption of perfect competition cannot be relaxed. Therefore, increasing returns to scale will invalidate the factor price equalization theorem.

(v) Different Production Functions in Different Countries

The factor price equalization theorem will be invalidated if the relationship between product prices and factor prices is no longer the same in all countries as a result of different production functions. This assumption cannot be relaxed either without invalidating the theorem.

(vi) Increasing Marginal Productivity of Factors

If production functions exhibit increasing marginal productivity of individual factors of production, it will no longer be true that the wage paid to the factor is equal to the marginal revenue product. Again, the direct link between factor productivity and factor remuneration required for factor price equalization will be broken.

(vii) Complete Specialization

One of the conditions for complete factor price equalization is that all countries will continue to produce all commodities after the introduction of international trade. In other words, complete specialization by a country will rule out the possibility of complete factor price equalization.[3]

Complete specialization will occur if the feasible regions of factor price changes for the two countries referred to in Section 6-2-a do not overlap. Such a case is illustrated in Figure 6-5. Here, the physical capital/labor endowment ratios in the United States and the United Kingdom differ markedly. Production and consumption patterns are such that the factor price ratios in the United States $(P_L/P_K)_{US}$ and the United Kingdom $(P_L/P_K)_{UK}$ are well within the feasible region before trade starts. After the opening up of trade relations, a world commodity price ratio $(P_W/P_C)_W$ will be established, and factor prices will *tend* toward equalization, which should *occur* at the factor price ratio $(P_L/P_K)_W$. However, due to the physical capital/labor ratios prevailing in the two countries, the movements of the factor prices toward

---

[3] Except in the borderline case where factor price equalization would be reached at precisely the same price ratios which would yield complete specialization.

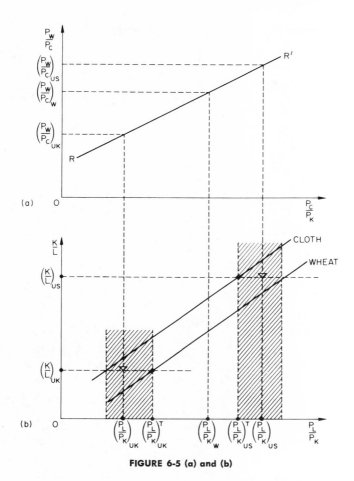

FIGURE 6-5 (a) and (b)

equalization will stop short of complete equalization. The factor price ratios are limited to the feasible regions indicated in Figure 6-5b, and as soon as the limits of the feasible regions are reached, the factor prices will stop moving. The new factor price ratios with trade are $(P_L/P_K)_{US}^T$ and $(P_L/P_K)_{UK}^T$ respectively. Both countries are completely specialized: the United States produces only cloth, and the United Kingdom produces only wheat.

After complete specialization is reached, the factor price ratios in the countries concerned can no longer adjust themselves to the ratio necessary for the attainment of complete factor price equalization.

(viii) Factor Intensity Reversals

It is possible for the factor intensities to be different in the relevant ranges of the production functions of the countries under consideration. Figure 6-6

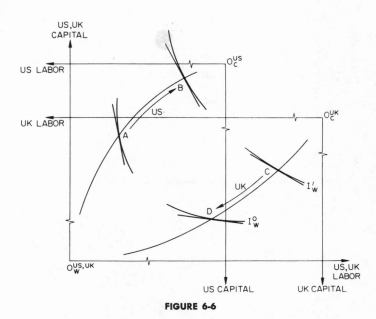

FIGURE 6-6

shows the Edgeworth Box diagrams for the United States and the United Kingdom. United States wheat production is shown as being capital intensive, while cloth production is labor intensive. The reverse holds true for the United Kingdom: wheat production is labor intensive and cloth production is capital intensive.

Let us assume that after the opening of trade relations the United States exports wheat and the United Kingdom exports cloth. This means that resources in the United States have to be reallocated from the contracting cloth industry to the expanding wheat industry. In the Edgeworth Box this is shown by the move from A to B. The price of the factor capital, which is used intensively in the expanding wheat industry, will increase. This is indicated by the slope of the price line tangent at B, which is flatter than the one at A. (Homogeneous isoquants allow us to make this comparison. See also Section 6-1 above.)

At the same time, the United Kingdom will expand her cloth production, which will drive up the price of capital because British cloth production is capital intensive. The slope of the price line tangent to the isoquants at point D is flatter than the one at point C. We can conclude that in the United Kingdom, just as in the United States, the price of capital has increased relatively to the price of labor. Because the factor price ratio moves in the same direction in both countries, it is in general not possible to determine whether the factor price gap will widen or will narrow with the introduction of international trade.

The case discussed here represents only one of many different possibilities which may arise if there are factor intensity reversals. Under certain circumstances a larger number of reversals will lead again to the narrowing of factor price gaps. But there is also the possibility that factor price differentials will increase after trade starts.

If there are factor intensity reversals within the relevant range of the production function, there may be a tendency for the factor price gap either to widen or to narrow, but complete equalization is ruled out.

(ix) Variable Factor Supplies

If the quantity of factors of production supplied is a function of the rate of return which these factors are able to obtain, factor price equalization will still take place after the markets have reached the new equilibrium point. This case will be discussed in greater detail in Section 6-3 below. Similarly, international factor mobility will be no obstacle to factor price equalization. As a matter of fact, if factors can move internationally in response to factor price differentials, these factor movements in themselves will tend to equalize factor prices. International trade is no longer necessary to produce factor price equalization, which can be accomplished directly by the factor movements.

(x) Tariffs and Transportation Costs

Tariffs and transportation costs are similar in their effect on product price equalization. We noted earlier that free international trade will lead to the establishment of identical product prices for all traded commodities. Tariffs and transportation costs will tend to make the prices paid by the residents of the exporting country lower than the prices paid by residents of the importing country. Product prices in different countries are no longer completely equalized by international trade. It follows that factor prices cannot be completely equalized either, because different product prices imply (given all our assumptions) different factor prices. We can say that with tariffs and transportation costs, there is still a *tendency* toward factor price equalization, without its being complete.

3. Factor Quantity Changes Caused by Trade

In the last section we showed the influence of international trade on factor prices. We assumed that the supply of the factors of production is perfectly inelastic. Changes in factor prices were not to influence the quantity of the factors of production supplied. Now we will assume that the factor supply curves are *not* perfectly inelastic. Under this new and less restrictive assumption, we can analyze the changes in the quantities of the factors that result from factor price changes induced by international trade.

a. Effects of Trade on Relative Factor Abundance

Except under unusual circumstances, as might occur with a demand reversal, we will find that the country exports the commodity which is intensive in her abundant factor. In the last section we saw that the price of the factor of production which is used relatively intensely in the export commodity will tend to rise. It follows that the price of the relatively abundant factor of production will tend to increase after trade starts.

If we assume now that factor quantities supplied are positively correlated with factor prices, we can conclude that increases in the factor prices

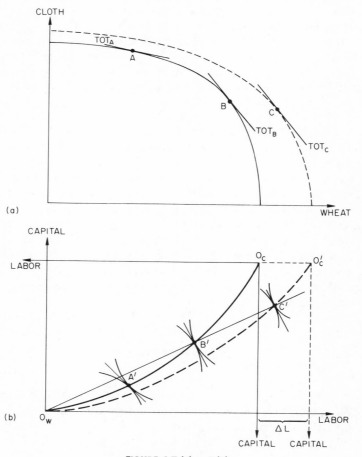

FIGURE 6-7 (a) and (b)

will bring forth increases in the factor quantities which are being supplied. As the factor prices of the already relatively abundant factor increase, the growing supplies of this factor will make it even more abundant.

Assuming homogeneous production functions, Figure 6-7b may help to illustrate the point. The graph shows the familiar box diagram, measuring quantities of inputs along the axes, and the line connecting all points of tangency for the different isoquants, namely, the contract curve. Let us assume that labor is the relatively abundant factor of our example. Free trade will lead to further specialization in the commodity which is intensive in the abundant factor, namely, wheat, and we will move from point A' to point B'. The labor/capital factor price ratio given by the slope of isoquants increases as we move from A' to B'. The higher price of labor will attract more workers, which represents a growth of the labor supply. Let us say that the box diagram increases by ΔL, moving the origin for cloth production to the new point O'_C.

We now have to find the point on the new contract curve (dashed line) at which the country will produce. To do this we recall that the factor price equalization theorem postulates a direct relationship between product prices and factor prices. The free trade product price ratio which corresponds to the factor price ratio at B' is the same as that which prevails after the factor supply adjustment has taken place.[4] Therefore the factor price ratio will be the same at the new point C' as it was at B'. Note that B' and C' are located on the same ray from the origin O_W. In a homogeneous isoquant set this assures identical factor price ratios.

As we move from B' to C', we find that wheat production expands and cloth production contracts. This is also shown in Figure 6-7a, which shows the production response to the factor price changes. We move from point A to point B before the factor quantity adjustment, and on to point C after the factor quantity has adjusted fully.

Specialization in production will be even stronger if we allow factor supplies to vary in response to induced factor price changes.

At first this may seem a surprising result, but when we consider that international trade tends to increase the price of the abundant factor, and that factor quantity changes help to keep this very factor price low, it is clear that a much greater expansion of the export industry's product is possible.

A few additional observations are in order. First of all, not only will the abundant factor of production expand in quantity, but the scarce factor, here capital, will tend to contract because its wage falls. Second, effects of trade on factor supplies will be similar in the other countries. Third, we can expect that product prices will not stay constant after the factor supplies have changed. It is not possible to make any generalizations about the direction

---

[4] This holds true in a strict sense only if the country under consideration is relatively small. The assumption will be dropped in the following chapter.

of the product price changes and their consequent effect on factor supplies. Some of the problems that come up in this connection will be discussed in Chapter 7, where we deal with problems of autonomous factor changes and their effects on international trade.

b. Effects of Changing Factor Supplies on the Production Possibility Curve

If we allow for the possibility of induced factor quantity changes, we have to address ourselves to the question of the effects of these factor quantity changes on the production possibility curve. We might be especially interested in the question of the position of the production possibility curve with constant factor supplies as opposed to the one with variable factor supplies.

In addition to the two commodities measured along the axes of the production possibility curve diagram, we introduce now a third variable: the changing factor supply. In order to keep the diagram to three dimensions, we will limit ourselves to the case of one factor of production only. In Figure 6-8

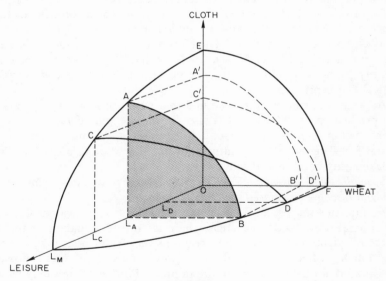

FIGURE 6-8

we measure leisure, the perfect complement to labor, along the third axis. Cloth is measured in the usual vertical direction and wheat in the horizontal direction. If the residents of the country should decide to consume all leisure available, i.e., 24 hours a day, 365 days a year, there would be no labor services provided at all, and, consequently, production will be equal to zero. The point in the figure corresponding to this state of affairs is L_M, where people consume the maximum amount of leisure possible. The production possibility curve has been reduced to a point. If, however, the residents of the country should work without interruption, consuming no leisure at all, we would find ourselves at point O of the diagram. Under these circumstances it is possible to produce anywhere on the production possibility curve EF.

In reality, we will find neither one of these two extreme possibilities. Let us start with the assumption of *fixed* factor supplies. The country's residents may want to consume OL_A of leisure and spend $L_A L_M$ of their total time on work. The production possibility curve corresponding to this work effort is labeled AB. Its projection on the cloth-wheat plane (dashed lines) is labeled A'B'. For each factor supply we can construct a corresponding production possibility curve, which can be visualized as a "slice" of the grand production possibility surface shown in Figure 6-8.

If we now allow for factor quantity changes in response to factor price changes induced by international trade, we may find that the total quantities of leisure demanded will vary between L_C and L_D. Corresponding to the varying amounts of work effort (equal to total time minus leisure time) are different points on the production possibility surface $L_M FE$ which are most preferred by the country. A set of such points is shown by the line CD. Note that at any point on CD the number of hours worked will be different. A projection of the variable factor supply production possibility curve CD on the cloth-wheat plane will generate C'D'.

The important observation to be made is that we are not able to make any general statements of the relationship of the fixed factor supply production possibility curve A'B' to the variable factor supply production possibility curve C'D'. These relationships will depend crucially on the trade-offs between cloth, wheat, and leisure which characterize the country.

The variable factor supply production possibility curve may lie wholly inside or wholly outside the fixed factor supply production possibility curve, or the two curves may intersect.

Two important policy conclusions emerge from the analysis in this chapter. For one, international trade will tend to eliminate factor price differentials that might exist between countries. Free international trade may thus serve as a full substitute for international factor movements, which would presumably also eliminate factor price differentials. Two, international trade tends to accentuate, rather than diminish, the relative domestic factor endowment ratios between countries. The relatively abundant factor of production will become even more abundant as a result of international trade. These two statements are not mutually inconsistent, as they might appear at first sight. The first statement refers to factor movements *between* countries, while the second is concerned with factor quantity changes *within* the same country. These latter factor *quantity* changes are caused by the very factor *price* changes that are the result of international trade.

4. Empirical Evidence

The most important problem discussed in this chapter is the possibility of international trade leading to factor price equalization. Much of the empirical evidence relevant for factor price equalization has been discussed in previous chapters, yet it might prove useful to assemble briefly the various bits of evidence which are of importance in this connection. We will concentrate attention on the assumptions which cannot be relaxed without invalidating the factor price equalization theorem.

a. Perfect Competition

Even casual armchair empiricism tells us that there are many industries which are not characterized by perfect competition. For this reason alone we should not expect complete factor price equalization to take place.

b. Returns to Scale

Evidence compiled by A. Walters and discussed in Section 3-2-a led us to the conclusion that the empirically relevant ranges of the production function are probably characterized by constant returns to scale. No obstacle to factor price equalization should be expected on this account.

c. Production Functions in Different Countries

Arrow, Chenery, Minhas, and Solow[5] found that production functions tend to differ between countries by a constant scale factor. As a result, factor price equalization cannot be expected to be complete in *absolute* terms. Yet, as the relative factor proportions used in the production of various commodities tend to be the same in different countries, we could still get an equalization of relative factor prices between countries. In other words, factor prices in different countries would differ by a constant factor, while their relative position to each other would be identical.

d. Marginal Productivity of Factors

There is no empirical evidence available which would point to the existence of increasing marginal productivity of factors of production, and we need expect no obstacle to factor price equalization from this source.

---

[5] K. Arrow, H. Chenery, B. Minhas, and R. Solow, "Capital-Labor Substitution and Economic Efficiency," *Review of Economics and Statistics*, August 1961.

e. Complete Specialization

There is a small number of commodities which are produced almost exclusively by one country. In most cases this is due to a virtual monopoly of resources required for their production. But patents or limited availability of relevant techniques and skills may also preserve the monopolistic position of one or a group of a few countries. Again, in these cases factor price equalization is not likely to occur.

f. Factor Intensity Reversals

Another important question, studied by B. S. Minhas,[6] is whether or not factor intensity reversals actually do occur within the empirically relevant ranges of the production function. For the United States Minhas found that these reversals do take place within the empirically relevant ranges, thus eliminating the possibility of factor price equalization.

From all the evidence presented it is clear that complete factor price equalization is unlikely. The most we can hope for is a *tendency* toward factor price equalization. But we must remember that we do not live in a static world where most variables do not change. The other factors at work may tend to increase, rather than narrow, the existing factor price gaps. The effect of international trade may be considered as a "leaning against the wind," in that factor price differentials would be even larger in the absence of trade.

SUGGESTED FURTHER READINGS

Balassa, Bela, "The Factor Price Equalization Controversy," *Weltwirtschaftliches Archiv*, No. 1, 1961.

Caves, Richard, *Trade and Economic Structure*. Cambridge: Harvard University Press, 1960, Chapter 3.

Heckscher, Eli, "The Effect of Foreign Trade on the Distribution of Income," *Ekonomisk Tidskrift*, 1919 (reprinted in H. Ellis and L. Metzler, *Readings in the Theory of International Trade*. Homewood, Ill.: Richard D. Irwin, 1950, Chapter 13).

Johnson, Harry, *International Trade and Economic Growth*. London: Allen & Unwin, 1958, Chapter 1.

Lancaster, Kelvin, "Protection and Real Wages: A Restatement," *Economic Journal*, June 1957.

[6] B. S. Minhas, "The Homohypallagic Production Function, Factor Intensity Reversals, and the Heckscher-Ohlin Theorem," *Journal of Political Economy*, April 1962.

Samuelson, Paul, "International Trade and the Equalization of Factor Prices" *Economic Journal*, June 1948.

Vanek, Jaroslav, "An Alternate Proof of the Factor Price Equalization Theorem," *Quarterly Journal of Economics*, November 1960.

————, *International Trade: Theory and Economic Policy*, Homewood, Ill.: Richard D. Irwin, 1962, pp. 205–211.

CHAPTER 7

Economic Growth
and International Trade

In the last chapter the effects of international trade on the factors of production were analyzed. We focused attention on changes in factor prices and factor supplies caused by the rearrangement of the production patterns made necessary after international trade was taken up. In this chapter we will follow the reverse procedure by taking factor supply changes as given and studying their effect on the pattern of international trade. In this context we will also investigate the question of what factor supply changes must take place if specific changes in trade patterns are to be achieved. This last area is particularly important in countries which are expanding and wish to ascertain whether economic growth will make them more dependent on international trade, or less. To simplify the analysis, we will assume throughout this chapter that factor prices stay constant.

1. The Small Country and Economic Growth

a. Consumption

A small country usually faces a given set of terms of trade at which she is able to exchange commodities. Let us assume initially that the country is characterized by constant cost conditions. Under these circumstances the country will specialize in the commodity in which she has a comparative advantage, say, wheat, and exchange some of her wheat output at the world terms of trade against cloth imports.

Before there is any economic growth the country is producing OA (Figure 7-1) of wheat. The international terms of trade are given by the slope of the

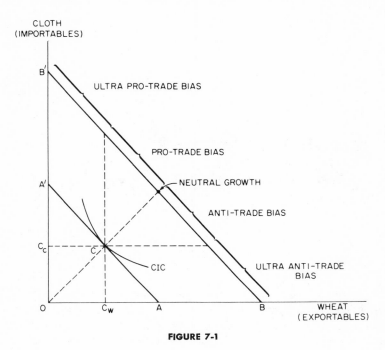

FIGURE 7-1

line AA', and in order to reach the highest possible community indifference curve, the country will modify her commodity bundle by exporting C_WA of wheat in exchange for C_WC of cloth. Thus she is able to attain commodity bundle C.

Now let economic growth occur, which will allow the country to produce the larger quantity of wheat OB. The now-attainable commodity combinations are delineated by the line BB', which describes the trading opportunities newly open to the country. The commodity bundle on BB' which will actually be chosen is, as usual, the one at which a community indifference curve is tangent to the price line.

The growth pattern of the country can be classified conveniently by using the relative size of the foreign trade sector as a yardstick. If its size in relation to total national output stays the same, we will speak of *neutral* economic growth. If it increases, we will speak of *pro-trade biased* economic growth. Conversely, a decrease in relative size will be referred to as an *anti-trade biased* growth. Finally, there is the possibility that not only the relative, but the *absolute*, size of the foreign trade sector increases more than the increase in national output. This will be called an *ultra pro-trade bias*. An absolute *decrease* in the foreign trade sector concomitant with economic growth will be referred to as an *ultra anti-trade bias*.

In the case of pro-trade biased, neutral, or anti-trade biased growth, part of the increase in income due to economic growth will be spent on the imported commodity. An ultra pro-trade bias occurs if the imported commodity is a superior good. Superior goods are characterized by the fact that people spend more than their income increase on the commodity. Similarly, the ultra anti-trade bias is the result of the imported commodity's being an inferior good; i.e., people spend an absolutely smaller amount on this commodity.

b. Production

Up to now we assumed that the growing country experiences constant opportunity costs in production, resulting in complete specialization in the commodity in which the country enjoys a comparative advantage. Here we may drop the constant cost assumption and assume instead that the country is characterized by increasing costs in production. This time we will attempt to isolate the effects of production patterns on economic self-sufficiency in the context of growth.

As before, the assumption crucial to our argument is that the terms of trade are given for the country in question. This given set of terms of trade is indicated by the slope of the line AA' in Figure 7-2. Given the initial production possibility curve TT', the country will produce at point P. Economic

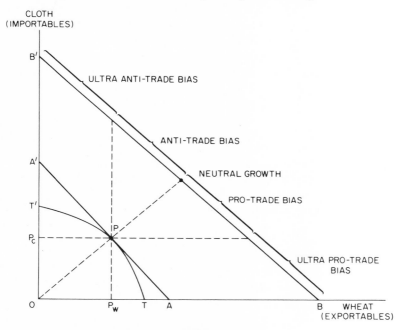

FIGURE 7-2

growth will lead to an outward shift of the production possibility curve. (Not shown in the diagram.) Again a tangency position of the production possibility curve to the terms of the trade will be found. If the new bundle of commodities to be produced contains more of the commodity which the country formerly imported, the country has become more self-sufficient. This growth pattern would therefore have had an *anti-trade* bias, because the volume of international trade has become smaller, relative to the total output. Again there exists the possibility of an *ultra anti-trade bias*, which will occur if the production of the importable commodity increases so strongly that the production of the other commodity actually decreases in absolute terms. In other words, if less than OP of wheat is produced (see Figure 7-2) as a result of economic growth, then growth is characterized by an ultra anti-trade bias. That is, of course, if cloth is the imported commodity. *Neutral* production increases take place if the output pattern does not change at all with economic growth. The relative shares of cloth and wheat produced stay constant. Finally, there remains the possibility of pro-trade biased growth. A *pro-trade bias* results from a country's producing a relatively (to total output) smaller amount of the imported commodity herself, while an *ultra pro-trade bias* implies that the country produces an absolutely smaller amount of the imported commodity after economic growth takes place. Thus the country becomes less self-sufficient, and hence the name pro-trade bias.

Hitherto we have not specified precisely how economic growth in the country occurred. Here two basic types of economic growth may be distinguished: (1) an increase in the factor quantities available, and (2) a technological advance, allowing production of a larger output with the same quantity of resources. We will discuss these two basic types of economic growth in turn.

(i) Factor Increases

A vital question for any growing country is how an increase in one or several factors of production will affect her output pattern, given a certain set of world prices. This question was investigated first by T. Rybczynski.[1] Let us first consider the case of an autonomous increase in one of the factors of production, and let us suppose that the labor force of the country increases due to population growth. In Figure 7-3b, the size of the box diagram will increase by the increase in the labor force (shown as dashed lines).

Before the increase in the labor force, the country was confined to the production possibility curve PP' (Figure 7-3a). Given the international terms of trade TOT, the country produced a commodity bundle A'. This output

---

[1] T. N. Rybczynski, "Factor Endowments and Relative Commodity Prices," *Economica*, November 1955.

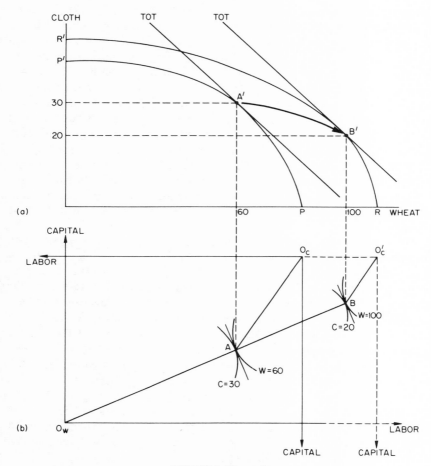

FIGURE 7-3 (a) and (b)

combination of 60 units of wheat and 30 units of cloth implies a resource allocation pattern indicated by point A in Figure 7-3b.

The increase in the work force will cause a shift in the production possibility curve from PP' to RR'. Given these expanded production possibilities, the country will again equal the terms of trade with the marginal rate of transformation. The new production point is B', where 100 units of wheat and 20 units of cloth are being produced.

At first it may seem surprising that economic growth of a factor of production will lead to a *decrease* in the output level of one product, while output of the other product increases, i.e., to an ultra-biased change in the production pattern. Our assumption that the country in question is so small that she faces a given set of world market prices, namely, the terms of trade TOT, is crucial here. We also know that under our usual set of assumptions, including linear homogeneous production functions, a unique relationship exists between product prices and factor prices. Therefore, since product prices do not change as a result of economic growth, the factor prices will have to stay the same, too. This, however, means that the factor intensities must also stay constant. In the Edgeworth Box shown in Figure 7-3b, the new equilibrium point B will have to lie on the same ray from the wheat origin as does point A. For the shifting origin of the isoquant system for cloth production, this condition is to be replaced by the requirement that the two rays depicting the factor intensities, i.e., AO_C and BO'_C, are parallel to each other. The only possible intersection of the factor intensity rays, namely, point B, will lie on a higher wheat isoquant and a lower cloth isoquant. The output of one commodity will therefore increase, while the output of the other will decrease in absolute amount.

We can go one step farther and infer from the foregoing analysis which product will be the one whose production increases and which one will decrease. In our example, wheat is relatively labor intensive, while cloth is relatively capital intensive. The additional workers have to be absorbed by the economy at the going wage for the reasons stated above. This can take place only if the additional workers are employed in the industry which uses labor intensively, and if *in addition* there is a decrease in the output level of the capital intensive industry. This latter decrease in output level will free relatively more capital than labor, and this capital can then be used together with the previously unemployed workers in the expanding wheat industry. The factor intensities can be maintained, too, because the expanding wheat industry uses relatively little capital. Thus it is clear that only an actual contraction of the cloth industry can free the capital required in the expanding wheat industry, such that the additional workers due to the labor force increase can find employment at the going wage.

An increase in one factor of production will lead to ultra biased growth, favoring the industry which uses the growing factor intensively.

Next we come to the case of biased economic growth. Actually, we will concentrate on the borderline case between ultra biased and biased growth, that is, the case of an increase in the output level of one product only. This kind of growth can be of great importance for a country wishing to pursue a development policy with a view to spurring output of only one commodity or group of commodities.

After the case of ultra biased growth, the answer to this problem is simple. We know that product prices will have to stay constant, and, consequently, factor prices cannot change either. In order to increase the output of one industry only, without affecting factor prices, factor quantities must be increased in precisely the same proportion as they are used in the industry in

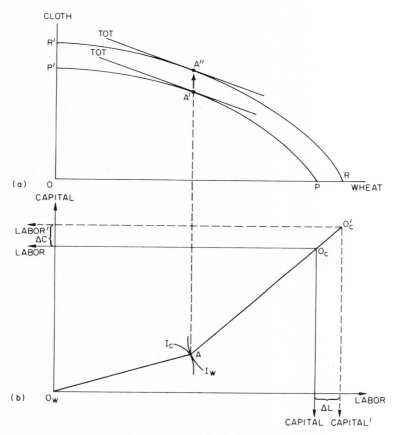

FIGURE 7-4 (a) and (b)

which expansion is to take place. Only under these conditions will there be no incentive for factors to migrate between the different industries.

Consider Figure 7-4. Production takes place initially at point A', and resource allocation patterns are depicted by point A. The aim is to expand output to a point like A'', where only cloth output is increased while wheat output remains the same as at point A'. As a result, it is necessary to stay on the same wheat isoquant in Figure 7-4b, while moving to a higher cloth isoquant. This must be done without changing the factor proportions used in either industry. The only way to accomplish this feat is to increase capital and labor by the amounts of ΔC and ΔL, which are exactly proportional to the factor intensity in the cloth industry. As a consequence, the origin for cloth production O_C in the Edgeworth Box will be displaced to O'_C. The cloth isoquant through point A will now denote a higher cloth output level because it is drawn with reference to an origin which is farther removed than it was before. The higher cloth isoquant denotes the new output level for cloth, shown by point A'' in the upper portion of the diagram.

An increase in factors of production in the same proportion as they are used in one industry will lead to an increase in the output level of that industry alone.

For various reasons it may be desirable to increase the outputs in exactly the same proportion as they are being produced at present. In other words, it may be desirable for economic growth to occur in a balanced or neutral pattern.

Again, product and factor prices will be the same before and after economic growth takes place. Thus the factor intensities in the production of both commodities cannot be affected. If, in addition, both outputs are to increase in exactly the same proportion as they did before economic growth occurred, the factors must be increased in accordance with a weighted average of their use in the two industries. This weighted average is provided by the *overall* capital/labor ratio which prevails in the country. All that is required, to attain neutral economic growth, is an increase of factors in exactly the proportion in which they are already applied in the country.

Figure 7-5 illustrates the point. The two factors of production are expanded in exactly the same proportion as they were used before economic growth occurs. The three points O_W, O_C, and O'_C are all located on a straight line. The condition of constancy of the factor prices requires again that the factor intensities stay the same, and the new resource allocation point B (Figure 7-5b) can be found by extending $O_W A$ beyond A, and drawing a line parallel to AO_C from the new origin O'_C. The intersection point of these two lines, point B, denotes the new resource allocation pattern. Given linear homogeneous production functions, the increase in the output of each one of the two commodities will be proportional to their original output level. In our example the output of both commodities is expanded by 50 per cent. Cloth production increases from 20 to 30 units, and wheat production expands from 30 to 45 units.

An increase of all factors of production in the proportion in which they are found in the economy will result in neutral economic growth.

(ii) Improvements in Technology

Economic growth, that is, an increase in the productive capacity of a country, results not only when the factors of production increase in quantity, but when there is an improvement in technology. The technological advance helps save resources, and the fixed resource endowment allows the country to produce a larger quantity of output.

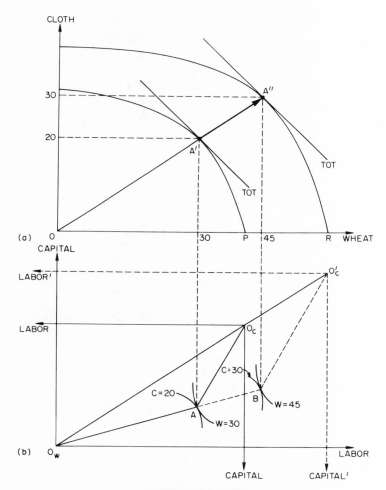

FIGURE 7-5 (a) and (b)

Now we have to distinguish carefully between two cases: (1) technological progress occurring in *both* industries in the same degree, and (2) technological progress occurring only in one industry.

Let us define as *neutral* technological progress an improvement in technology which saves all factors of production to the same extent. If such neutral technological progress takes place simultaneously in both industries, we find that each isoquant is now associated with a higher level of output than before. The same amount of resources can produce a larger quantity of output no matter in which industry the resources are employed. The result is that output levels of both industries increase proportionally. Given the assumption of fixed world prices, the production pattern of the country will expand in a neutral fashion, i.e., the wheat/cloth output mix will be unaffected. Note that while world *prices* have remained constant, per unit *costs* of production have fallen, thus leading to higher profit margins in both industries. But as the profitability of both industries increases to the same extent, there is no incentive to shift resources from one industry to the other.

Neutral technological progress in all industries will lead to a proportional expansion of all industries.

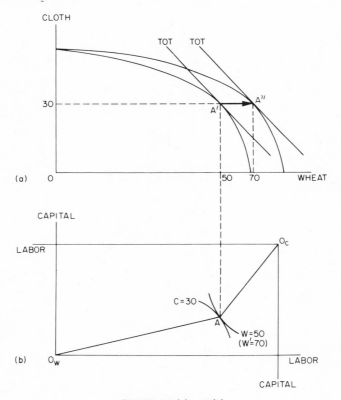

FIGURE 7-6 (a) and (b)

The situation is quite different if the neutral technological progress occurs in only one industry. (See Figure 7-6.) In this case the *cost* of production will decrease in this industry alone, while world *prices* remain unchanged. The result is that only in the industry experiencing technological progress are profit margins increased, while they remain at their old level in the other industry. Consequently, there will be a shift of resources to the industry experiencing the technological progress, expanding its output level even more, while the other industry has to contract because resources are being with-drawn.

Neutral technological progress in one industry alone will lead to an expansion of this industry, while the other industry will contract.

In the case of biased technological progress, the situation is still different. The word biased refers here to an improvement in technology which economizes on the use of the factors of production in different proportions. We will assume that the biased technological progress occurs only in the wheat indus-

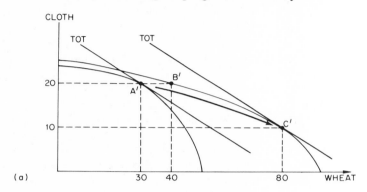

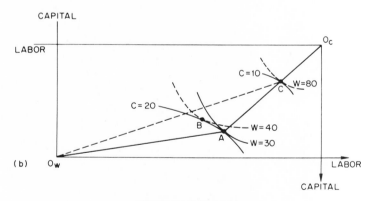

FIGURE 7-7 (a) and (b)

try. If it is also stipulated that the factor prices are not to be changed, this means that the cloth industry, where no technological change has occurred, will continue to operate with the same capital/labor ratio as before. In other words, the cloth industry is confined to the factor intensity ray which emanates from O_C and passes through A (see Figure 7-7b).

Now let us turn to the wheat industry and assume that the biased technological progress is of the labor-saving variety. In our example, labor is the factor of production which is used intensively in the wheat industry. As this factor is saved, some of the workers in the wheat industry will no longer be able to find employment at the going wage. The wheat industry will want to employ a larger quantity of capital in conjunction with each worker.

This point is illustrated in Figure 7-7b, where production is assumed to take place initially at point A, leading to a cloth output of 20 units and a wheat output of 30 units. After the labor-saving technological improvement occurs, the new (dashed) isoquants will represent the production function for wheat. Point B is an efficient point of production now, because it shows a point at which a new wheat isoquant is tangent to a cloth isoquant. However, point B violates one of our initial stipulations, that the factor price ratio remain unchanged. Also, the factor intensity ratio in the cloth industry is different from the initial situation.

To restore the original factor price ratio, the workers who were "saved" in the wheat industry due to the technological advance must get the same proportion of capital to work with as before. This required capital can be obtained only through a contraction of the capital-intensive cloth industry. As the cloth industry contracts, it releases relatively more capital than labor. This capital can be used in the wheat industry, which is expanding, in order to restore the marginal productivity—and by this the wage—of the factor labor.

The final point of equilibrium is shown by C, which is the point of tangency of a cloth isoquant (C = 10) and a new wheat isoquant (W = 80). The factor price ratio at C is the same as at A, because both are located on the same ray from the origin O_C. The homogeneity assumption about the isoquants assures that all the cloth isoquants have the same slope at the point at which they are cut by the ray. After the labor-saving technological improvement, the wheat industry will use *relatively* less labor. The absolute amount of both factors of production in the wheat industry will increase, as will the output level.

Technological progress which saves the factor of production used intensively in that industry will lead to ultra biased growth of this industry.

There is one other case which should be examined in this context. If technological progress in the wheat industry saves the factor of production that is used relatively little, i.e., capital, it will be found that this capital can be absorbed at the going wage only in the other industry. The cloth industry which uses capital intensively will therefore expand. The wheat industry, in which the technological progress occurs, is also likely to expand somewhat. In general, however, it will not be possible to say whether the resulting economic growth is biased in favor of one or the other industry. All we can tell is that it will not be ultra biased.

Technological progress which saves the factor of production which is not used intensively in that industry will lead to growth of both industries.

c. Net Effects of Growth

Neither production effects nor consumption effects alone decide whether economic growth occurring in a country is going to be neutral, biased, or even ultra biased. To determine the final effects of growth one has to take both consumption and production patterns of the growing country into consideration. The *net effect* of changes in consumption and production patterns due to economic growth will determine the effects of growth on the size of the foreign trade sector.

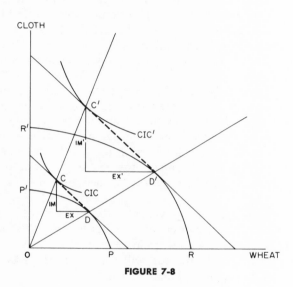

FIGURE 7-8

Figure 7-8 shows some of the relevant magnitudes. In the graph the production pattern before the occurrence of economic growth is given by D, and a neutral growth pattern brings us to point D' after growth has occurred. Similarly, there is a movement from consumption point C to C' due to growth. The net effect in the example shown is that trade expands in exact proportion to the growth in national income. The dashed lines show the exports and imports traded by the country at the different levels of total output.

The only observation which can be made regarding the size of the foreign trade sector is that essentially anything is possible. Even an ultra pro-trade biased growth in consumption might be turned by a strongly ultra anti-trade biased growth in production into an ultra anti-trade bias as far as the net results are concerned. Only if more specific assumptions as to the likely magnitude of the different effects are made will it be possible to narrow down the range of possible outcomes. To give a complete taxonomy of all the possible cases would, however, lead us too far astray.

2. The Large Country and Economic Growth

Throughout the preceding discussion it was assumed that the country is relatively small and faces a given set of terms of trade at which it can trade any quantity of commodities desired. This condition will be replaced now by the assumption that the country is significantly large, so that international terms of trade will in fact be influenced by her actions. Most of the conclusions established in the preceding pages will no longer hold true and must be modified to take account of the changing international commodity prices caused by economic growth.

Here we will deal only with the net effects of economic growth on the country. Pro-trade biased economic growth is again taken to mean that the country will demand a larger quantity of imports in exchange for a larger quantity of exports, thus increasing the aggregate trade volume. Consequently, the price of imports will be driven up and the price of exports will fall. The terms of trade turn "against" the country, because only a smaller quantity of imports can now be obtained for the same (or even larger) quantity of exports.

With an anti-trade bias it is possible for the terms of trade to turn either in favor of or against the growing country. The criterion in this case is whether the *absolute* quantity of trade tends to increase or to decrease concomitantly to economic growth. The final result will depend on the elasticities of the domestic and foreign supply and demand curves.

Even with a neutral trade biased growth there exists the possibility that the terms of trade may turn so strongly against the growing country that she will actually wind up on a lower indifference curve than she could attain before economic growth. This case of immizerizing growth,[2] as it is often called, is illustrated in Figure 7-9. Production takes place initially at point P_1, and the country consumes the commodity combination C_1. Thus she is able to reach the community indifference curve CIC_1. After economic growth occurs, production changes to P_2, and as the terms of trade change to TOT_2, the best possible consumption point is C_2. Point C_2, however, is located on the community indifference curve CIC_0, which is located below the community indifference curve CIC_1 and therefore denotes a lower attainable welfare level. The country will be worse off as a consequence of economic growth.

We should point out, though, that it is always possible for the growing country to levy an appropriate tariff, which will protect the country from

---

[2] J. Bhagwati, "Immizerizing Growth," *Review of Economic Studies*, June 1958.

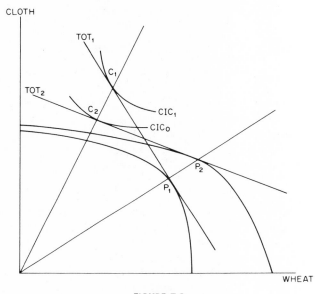

FIGURE 7-9

welfare losses it would otherwise experience. This becomes clear when we recall that the offer curve of the trading partner has not changed at all because of the economic growth in the large country. Foreigners will always be willing to continue to exchange the same quantity of commodities at the old terms of trade.

Economic growth in a large country which increases the volume of trade may lead to a deterioration of the terms of trade. The terms of trade may deteriorate to such an extent that the country is worse off as a result of growth. This, however, can always be avoided by the imposition of an appropriate tariff.

The policy implications of this conclusion can be observed frequently. To avoid the deterioration of the terms of trade caused by the sale of larger quantities of a country's export commodity, especially in the face of inelastic demand curves, the country can assess export duties on the commodity. Quantitative restrictions are employed frequently with the same result. As home demand for the commodities involved may be insufficient, it may even be rational from the viewpoint of the exporting country to place limitations on the production of the commodity or, if it is a perishable commodity and has been produced already, to destroy it.

3. Empirical Evidence

The basic question of this chapter is whether the foreign trade sector tends to grow proportionally faster or slower than national output as a whole.

Does economic growth make a country more dependent on foreign trade, or less?

Empirical evidence on this topic is hard to come by, and the few available studies present only fragmentary evidence. In several time series studies of the share of foreign trade in national income, Karl Deutsch and Alexander Eckstein[3] conclude that there is a tendency for international trade to expand relatively to national income in the early stages of industrialization. After this, however, there seems to be a persistent decline in the percentage of foreign traded commodities. The peak in the size of the foreign trade sector seems to come for most countries with the completion of industrialization. For most of the European countries it can be placed in the late nineteenth and early twentieth centuries.

This evidence on the share of foreign trade in world income is supported by the finding that the growth rate of exports lags persistently behind the growth rate for national income for ten countries which account for more than 50 per cent of total world trade.

We are able to assemble some evidence on why the share of foreign trade relative to income tends to decline. For one, agricultural products are characterized by inelastic demand patterns, as was pointed out in Section 4-3. As income levels go up, the demand for these items increases less than proportionally, and to the extent that they are traded internationally, trade will tend to decrease relatively to national income.

A second important influence is the tendency for services to increase as the income level goes up. As the bulk of all services is of the domestic variety, an increase in the service sector goes hand in hand with a decline of the foreign trade sector. The most important international service is foreign travel.

Finally, industrial growth tends to occur in most countries at a more rapid rate than the increase in demand.[4] As a consequence we find that countries will tend to substitute their own industrial products for imports. The result is a further decline in the importance of the foreign trade sector in relation to total national income. Chenery found that even in Japan, one of the countries most successful in expanding exports, 40 per cent of industrial growth was due to import substitution while only 10 per cent was due to increased exports.

We can conclude that on both the consumption and production sides there exists an anti-trade bias in the growth pattern of most countries, once they have reached a stage at which they are industrialized. But it should be pointed out again that the evidence presented here is far from complete and

---

[3] K. Deutsch and A. Eckstein, "National Industrialization and the Declining Share of the International Economic Sector, 1890–1959," *World Politics*, January 1961.

[4] H. Chenery, "Patterns of Industrial Growth," *American Economic Review*, September 1960.

that much further research needs to be done before we can hope to state the relationships between economic growth and international trade in a more definite manner.

SUGGESTED FURTHER READINGS

Bhagwati, Jagdish, "Immizerizing Growth," *Review of Economic Studies*, June 1958.

Caves, Richard, *Trade and Economic Structure*. Cambridge: Harvard University Press, 1960, Chapter 4.

Johnson, Harry, *International Trade and Economic Growth*. London: Allen & Unwin, 1958, Chapters 3 and 4.

———, *Money, Trade, and Economic Growth*. Cambridge: Harvard University Press, 1962, Chapter 4.

Kemp, Murray, *The Price Theory of International Trade*. Englewood Cliffs, N.J.: Prentice-Hall, 1964, Chapter 7.

Meier, Gerald, *International Trade and Development*. New York: Harper & Row, 1963, Chapter 2.

Mundell, Robert, "International Trade and Factor Mobility," *American Economic Review*, June 1957.

Rybczynski, T. M., "Factor Endowments and Relative Commodity Prices," *Economica*, November 1955.

CHAPTER 8

Welfare Aspects
of Free Trade

We have thus far been concerned mainly with the reasons for international trade. Differences in demand patterns, technology, or factor endowments between countries were cited as some of the factors leading to the emergence of international trade. But, clearly, countries and people would have no incentive to engage in international trade if it were not going to make them better off. Increases in economic welfare make international trade attractive, and it is therefore important to show in greater detail the effects of international trade on economic welfare.

It is again necessary to find an appropriate measurement by which to judge whether a change in an economic situation has in fact made an economic unit better off or worse off. The measure to be used for this purpose is the community indifference curve concept which was developed in detail in Section 4-1. At that time we enumerated several possible justifications for the use of community indifference curves. These were: (1) that the country is inhabited by one person only; (2) that a benevolent dictator defines a unique set of communal preferences; (3) that all residents have the same incomes and tastes; (4) that all residents are characterized by the same tastes and that they have homogeneous indifference curves; (5) that all residents have the same income and homogeneous indifference curves; and (6) that some income redistribution scheme maintains a socially optimal income distribution pattern. All but one of these justifications can be used if we want the community indifference curves to act as a welfare indicator. The one exception is justification (4), which specified identical tastes and homogeneous indifference curves. Under these circumstances it is possible for one resident (or group of residents) to be made better off while another group is worse off because of a change in the economic situation. In general, no interpersonal utility comparisons of this sort are admissible, and for this reason we shall delete (4) from the list of justifications for the use of community indifference curves for welfare analysis.

We will start out with an investigation of the effects of trade on world welfare without paying attention to the welfare of individual countries. Then we will proceed to analyze the effects of trade on the welfare of the individual country. Finally, we will concern ourselves with the effects of trade on economic groups within a country engaging in international trade.

1. World Welfare

It can be shown that unrestricted international trade increases welfare for the world as a whole. That is, aggregate world welfare can be increased disregarding for the moment how the possible gains (or losses) from international trade are distributed between different countries.

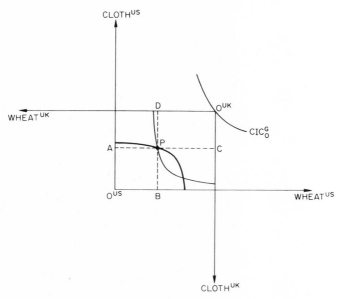

FIGURE 8-1

In Figure 8-1 the production possibility curve of the United States is shown in its customary position. Quantities of cloth and wheat are measured along the two axes. Let us say that taste patterns are such that production and consumption will occur at point P. The United States will be producing and consuming AO^{US} of cloth and BO^{US} of wheat. A similar production possibility curve can be drawn for the United Kingdom and superimposed on the original diagram upside down and with sides reversed. Furthermore, the British production and consumption point is placed so that it coincides with the United States production and consumption point P. The United Kingdom produces DO^{UK} of wheat and CO^{UK} of cloth.

The total production for the world, which consists only of our two countries, is given by the size of the resulting box diagram, or is equal to AO^{US} plus CO^{UK} of cloth and DO^{UK} plus BO^{US} of wheat. With reference to the original (United States) coordinate system, the point O^{UK} shows the total commodity combinations that are being produced and consumed in the world as a whole. The two countries together can attain a welfare level indicated by the global community indifference curve passing through O^{UK}, i.e., the indifference curve CIC_0^G.

It will be noted that at point P the marginal rate of transformation of cloth into wheat in the United States is not equal to that of the United Kingdom. This gives us an indication that resource allocation in the world as a whole is not to be considered optimal.

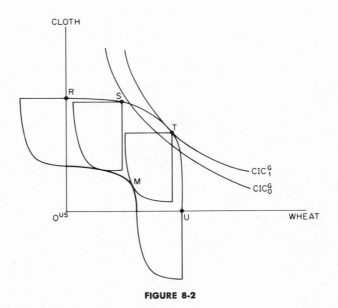

FIGURE 8-2

Total world production can be increased if the two countries rearrange their production patterns in such a way that they will lead to equality of the marginal rates of transformation between the two countries. This condition will be fulfilled if the two production possibility curves are tangent to each other. Such a position is shown in Figure 8-2, where the two countries' production possibilities curves are tangent to each other at point M. Naturally, there are other production patterns which will lead to the equality of the marginal rates of transformation, too. These different possible product combinations can be attained by sliding the British production possibility curve along the United States production possibility curve in such a way that the coordinate systems of the two countries are always parallel to each other. Several possible situations are shown in Figure 8-2.

Measuring with reference to the original (United States) coordinate system, we find that the origin of the shifting (British) production possibility curve traces out the *aggregate* commodity combinations which can be produced in the two countries together. The aggregate amounts delineate the production possibilities for the world as a whole; the moving origin of the British production possibility curve traces, therefore, the world production possibility curve. This world production possibility curve is labeled RSTU.

The world production possibility curve RSTU will allow the world as a whole to reach the global community indifference curve CIC_1^G lying above the global community indifference curve CIC_0^G, which could be reached with both countries maintaining autarky.

For the world as a whole, a free trade situation leads to a higher level of economic welfare than a situation in which there is no international trade.

It may be worth noting that in the very special case in which production and consumption patterns in both countries lead to the same marginal rate of transformation even in the absence of trade, the total amounts produced by the two countries in isolation will actually be a point on the world production possibility curve. In such a case domestic price ratios are already equal before trade starts, and there is no incentive to engage in international trade. The countries in isolation are as well off as they can be.

2. A Country's Welfare

We have demonstrated that it is advantageous for the world as a whole to engage in international trade, because all countries together are able to achieve a higher aggregate utility level as indicated by the higher global community indifference curve which can be reached. Yet this does not permit us to draw any conclusions about the welfare of the individual countries concerned. It might be that the gain is distributed in some inequitable fashion between the two countries; it might be that one country reaps all the benefits, leaving the other country just as well off as it was without trade; or one country might even experience a gain in welfare larger than the aggregate increase in welfare for the world as a whole. In the latter case the other country would actually experience a decrease in utility because of the opening up of trade relations.

a. A Small Country's Welfare

Let us suppose initially that the country under consideration is relatively small. As before, this country's actions are not likely to influence the international terms of trade, which she considers as given.

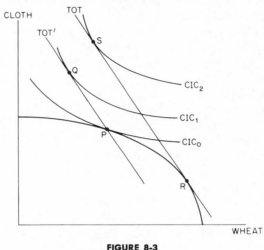

FIGURE 8-3

Figure 8-3 shows the production possibility curve of such a small country. Under conditions of autarky the commodity bundles which the country can attain are limited to those commodity combinations depicted by points on or below the production possibility curve. The highest possible community indifference curve which the country can reach is curve CIC_0, tangent to the country's production possibility curve at point P.

By allowing the small country to trade at the fixed terms of trade TOT, the country can reach any commodity combination which lies on or below the international terms of trade line. Thus she is able to attain commodity combinations which contain more of *both* commodities than could be produced under autarky. It is clear that given the possibility of obtaining larger commodity combinations via trade, she is also able to reach a higher community indifference curve, such as CIC_2.

The ability to attain a higher community indifference curve indicates that free trade has made the country as a whole better off, and constitutes, therefore, an improvement in economic welfare for this country. It is immaterial that the terms of trade line is either steeper or flatter than the price line showing the pretrade domestic exchange ratio. In either case the country will find that the attainable commodity combinations with international trade are greater than the commodity combinations that can be produced in isolation at home.

The total gain from trade which the country derives can be subdivided into the gains from exchange and the gains from specialization. The *gains from exchange* accrue to the country because she is able to trade internationally and to modify the commodity bundle which she produces under autarky. To isolate these gains from exchange, we may assume that the production pattern of the country remains the same as under autarky. Thus the country continues to produce at point P. However, she can now modify the commodity bundle by trading at the terms of trade that prevail in the world market. (Note that TOT' is parallel to TOT.) Thus she is able to reach the higher community indifference curve CIC_1. This movement represents the welfare gain from exchange.

The country also gains *from specialization* in production. At the new terms of trade the marginal rate of transformation is no longer equal to the price ratio of the two commodities. It is advantageous for the country to rearrange her production pattern in such a way that the marginal rate of transformation is equal to the international price ratio. In Figure 8-3 this is true at point R, where the terms of trade line TOT is tangent to the production possibility curve. The country is able to reach an even higher community indifference curve, CIC_2, and the consequent welfare increase can be attributed to the gains from specialization.

The total welfare gain realized by the movement from indifference curve CIC_0 to CIC_2 made possible by international trade can thus be decomposed into the gains from exchange (CIC_0 to CIC_1) and the gains from specialization (CIC_1 to CIC_2).

b. A Large Country's Welfare[1]

If the country under consideration is relatively large, the assumption that the international terms of trade at which the country can trade will remain constant is no longer valid. As soon as the large country enters the international market, her trading activities will tend to drive up the price of her imports and lower the price of her exports. For this reason the trading opportunities of the large country can no longer be represented by a straight line showing the terms of trade prevailing in the world market. Instead, new means must be found to represent the commodity combinations attainable by trade, which we shall refer to as the *trade possibilities curve*.

In Figure 8-4 PABCP is the production possibility curve for the United States. The insert shows the foreign trade offer curve for the United Kingdom,

[1] The rest of this section (up to page 135) may be skipped without affecting continuity.

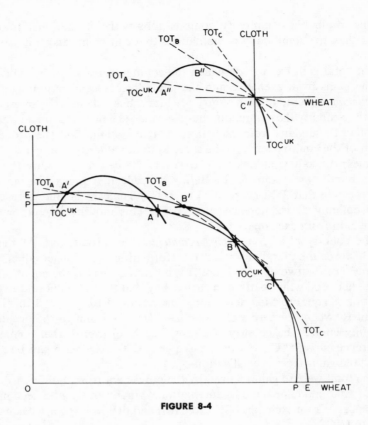

FIGURE 8-4

including several different possible terms of trade. The first step in the construction of the trade possibilities curve for the United States is to assume any arbitrary terms of trade, say, TOT_A, and to place the origin of the British coordinate system in such a position that the terms of trade line TOT_A is tangent to the United States production possibility curve. For the terms of trade TOT_A this is true at point A. The British offer curve shows the willingness of the United Kingdom to trade, and, given the terms of trade TOT_A, indicates that she will want to move to point A'.

The process has to be repeated now for every conceivable terms of trade ratio, such as TOT_B. Again the British origin is placed on the United States production possibility curve so that the terms of trade line TOT_B is tangent to the production possibility curve. At the new terms of trade the United Kingdom will want to move to point B'. It is possible to generate a whole set of points showing the United Kingdom's willingness to trade with the United States, and the line connecting all such points, EA'B'CE, shows the commodity combinations which are attainable for the *United States* by trading

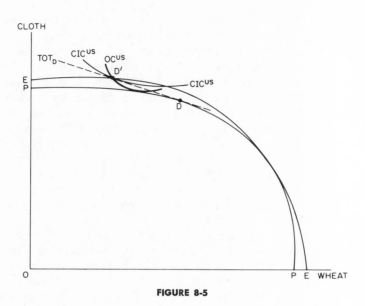

FIGURE 8-5

with the United Kingdom. EA'B'CE delineates, therefore, the United States trade possibility curve.

In Figure 8-5 we reproduce the production possibility curve PP and the trade possibility curve EE for the United States. In addition, we show the customary offer curve for the United States, OC^{US}, which is arrived at by confronting the United States with all possible terms of trade and observing the amounts which she wants to trade. At the terms of trade TOT_D she will want to produce at point D and trade to attain commodity combination D'. At D' the United States reaches the highest possible community indifference curve, here shown as CIC^{US}.

The equilibrium international terms of trade are reached when trade between the two countries is balanced. Clearly, this requires that the terms of trade pass through the point of intersection of the trade possibilities curve EE and the offer curve OC^{US}. In the figure the equilibrium terms of trade are shown as TOT_D. This follows from the fact that the trade possibility curve is constructed by observing the trade patterns that the United Kingdom chooses at any given terms of trade. Given the terms of trade of our example, a placing of the origin of the British coordinate system at point D would result in a British offer curve which passes through D'.

The trade possibilities curve can now be used to show the commodity combinations that are attainable for a large country engaging in free international trade. Since this curve lies above the production possibility curve at all points (except for the point at which they coincide), we can conclude that free trade will also permit the large country to attain a greater commodity combination than could be attained without trade. For any given commodity bundle that could be produced in isolation, a commodity bundle containing more of *both* commodities could always be found with the introduction of free trade. Since a commodity bundle containing more of both commodities will always be located on a higher community indifference curve than a bundle containing less of both commodities, it is possible to state unambiguously that free trade will always lead to an improvement in economic welfare.

Free international trade will make it possible for the country as a whole to achieve a higher level of welfare than can be achieved under autarky. The gains in welfare are due to gains from exchange and gains from specialization.

The foregoing analysis has shown that with a given amount of resources, free trade makes possible the attainment of a higher level of welfare than does a no-trade situation. As a corollary it can be demonstrated that a *given* level of welfare can be attained with a *smaller* productive effort if the country is allowed to trade. In Figure 8-6 we show the production possibility curve and community indifference curve of a small country. The country produces and consumes at point P in isolation. Now the possibility of international exchange is introduced at the terms of trade TOT. If the country wants to remain on indifference curve CIC, she is able to do so at point R. In order to get to R, she must produce a commodity combination anywhere along the terms of trade line which will allow her to modify the produced commodity bundle by trade to commodity bundle R. All points between S and T on the terms of trade line are attainable by production, given the production possibilities, and all these points lie below the production possibilities curve itself, indicating that they can be reached without the full use of available productive resources. The productive resources which are no longer required to

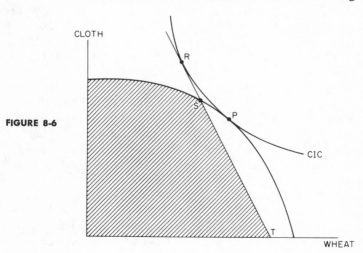

FIGURE 8-6

attain the indifference curve CIC can now be used for other purposes: they may be diverted to the construction of capital goods, making future consumption possibilities greater, or they may be taken in the form of leisure or something else.

Free trade will allow a country to reach a given level of welfare with a smaller resource combination than would be required under autarky.

In Chapter 9 it will be shown that a country which possesses a certain degree of monopoly power and is willing to use it may increase its own welfare above the level of welfare achieved with free trade. Similarly, countries which collaborate by forming a customs union may be able to reap additional gains under certain circumstances, as will be demonstrated in Chapter 10.

3. The Welfare of an Economic Group

While we previously analyzed the gains which accrue to the world as a whole and to individual countries engaging in free international trade, we will now address ourselves to the changes in economic welfare which may be experienced by one economic group within a country.

a. Specialized Factors of Production

It is easily seen that a factor which is completely specialized in the production of the commodity in which the country has a comparative *dis*advantage will suffer if the country engages in free international trade. This is because after the opening of trade the country will specialize in, and therefore expand the production of, the product in which it has a comparative advantage. Simultaneously, the country will reduce production of the product in which it has a comparative disadvantage. If there is a factor of production which is specialized in the production of this latter commodity, it will be impossible for this factor to find employment in the expanding industries. In such a case the specialized factor will experience a reduction in its economic welfare.

b. Mobile Factors of Production (The Stolper-Samuelson Theorem)[2]

More interesting than the case of a completely specialized factor of production is the case of a broad group of *un*specialized factors. We may think in this context of aggregate factor groups like land, labor, and capital, and we will assume that these factors of production are free to move between different employments. Our usual catalogue of assumptions as given in Section 6-2 is assumed to hold.

[2] See W. Stolper and P. Samuelson, "Protection and Real Wages," *Review of Economic Studies*, November 1941.

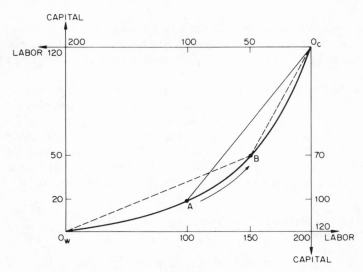

FIGURE 8-7

In Figure 8-7 we show the Edgeworth Box diagram for the country. Inputs of labor and capital are measured along the axes. Before trade starts, the country produces at point A on her contract curve; after trade opens up, she rearranges her factors of production so that she will be able to produce at point B, also located on the contract curve. Wheat production, which is labor intensive in our example, expands, while the capital-intensive cloth production contracts.

The contracting cloth industry will release relatively more capital than will be absorbed at the going wage rate in the expanding wheat industry. In order to find employment, the capital wage will have to fall. At the same time the expanding wheat industry will want to employ more workers than can be hired at the going wage. Consequently, the wage of labor will be driven up. The *relative* wage of the factor used intensively in the contracting industry will fall, while the relative wage of the factor used intensively in the expanding industry will rise.

Owing to the relative factor price changes, making capital cheaper, *both* industries will tend to employ more capital. As the total amount of labor is fixed in our model, each unit of capital will have a smaller quantity of labor to work with. Under conditions of perfect competition, each factor is paid the value of its marginal product. But the marginal productivity of a factor is absolutely lower if the quantity of other factors in conjunction with which it works is lowered. As the marginal productivity of capital decreases absolutely, capital will be paid an *absolutely* lower wage. This is true in both industries, and must therefore be true for all units of capital within the country.

The reverse argument applies to the factor which is used intensively in the expanding industry: labor. Each worker will have a larger quantity of capital to work with, increasing labor's productivity and increasing its absolute wage in both industries.

It may seem paradoxical at first that the capital/labor ratio in both industries can increase while the overall capital/labor ratio for the country as a whole stays constant. The solution to this apparent inconsistency is found in the fact that the overall capital/labor ratio is a weighted average of the two industries. As the relative size of the industries changes, the weights change, too. If the weight assigned to the industry with the higher capital/labor ratio decreases, while the weight of the industry with the lower capital/labor ratio increases, it is possible for the overall ratio to stay constant. This can easily be seen from Table 8-1, where the numerical values of the capital/labor ratios corresponding to Figure 8-7 are shown.

TABLE 8-1

		Wheat	Cloth	Overall
Capital / Labor	Before Trade	$\frac{20}{100} = \frac{.2}{1}$	$\frac{100}{100} = \frac{1}{1}$	$\frac{120}{200}$
Capital / Labor	After Trade	$\frac{50}{150} = \frac{.33}{1}$	$\frac{70}{50} = \frac{1.4}{1}$	$\frac{120}{200}$

It is evident that the capital/labor ratio in both the wheat and the cloth industry has increased after international trade is introduced, while the aggregate quantities have stayed constant.

Finally, it remains to be observed that as the total quantity of capital and labor remains unchanged, an increase in the absolute wage received by each worker will lead to an absolutely larger wage bill for all workers together. At the same time the lower absolute wage of capital means that the absolute amount received by owners of the factor of production capital will decrease. A larger absolute wage bill received by a factor will allow the owners of this factor to achieve a higher level of welfare, since the larger wage bill permits the purchase of an absolutely larger commodity bundle.

International trade will increase the level of welfare of the owners of the factor of production which is used intensively in the expanding industry; the owners of the factor used intensively in the contracting industry will be worse off.

The argument of this section shows that the opposition of individual economic groups within a country to a change in trade policy may well be justified, if these economic groups are the ones that are actually going to be hurt. Yet it should be noted that our conclusion that the country as a whole will be better off still holds. Consequently, we find that the gains realized by one economic group consist essentially of two parts: (1) the gains which accrue to the country as a whole, and which are reaped by the gainers, and (2) the losses which are experienced by the other economic group, and which must (in our two-factor model) be reaped by the gainers, too. If the owners of the gaining factor of production were to compensate the owners of the losing factor for the losses suffered, there must still be some additional gains left for the owners of the gaining factor. It must therefore be true that some residents of a country engaging in international trade can be made better off without their making someone else worse off, if proper compensation is paid by the gainers to the losers. Note that we are able to avoid interpersonal utility comparisons by requiring the losers to be reimbursed only for their losses. Thus the income transfers mentioned as the second part of the welfare gain realized by the gainers are eliminated. There are still additional gains mentioned under (1) which accrue to the gainers. If some people are made better off without anybody else being made worse off, we can conclude that there has been an improvement in economic welfare.

SUGGESTED FURTHER READINGS

Baldwin, Robert, "The New Welfare Economics and Gains in International Trade," *Quarterly Journal of Economics*, February 1952.

Caves, Richard, *Trade and Economic Structure*. Cambridge: Harvard University Press, 1960, Chapter 8.

Corden, Max, "Recent Developments in the Theory of International Trade," *Special Papers in International Economics*, No. 7, International Finance Section, Princeton University, 1965, Chapter 4.

Samuelson, Paul, "The Gains from International Trade," *Canadian Journal of Economics and Political Science*, May 1939 (reprinted in H. Ellis and L. Metzler, *Readings in the Theory of International Trade*. Homewood, Ill.: Richard D. Irwin, 1950, Chapter 11).

———, "The Gains from International Trade Once Again," *Economic Journal*, December 1962.

———, "Welfare Economics and International Trade," *American Economic Review*, June 1938.

Stolper, W., and P. Samuelson, "Protection and Real Wages," *Review of Economic Studies*, November 1941 (reprinted in H. Ellis and L. Metzler, *Readings in the Theory of International Trade*. Homewood, Ill.: Richard D. Irwin, 1950, Chapter 15).

Vanek, Jaroslav, *International Trade: Theory and Economic Policy*. Homewood, Ill.: Richard D. Irwin, 1962, Chapter 15.

CHAPTER 9

Tariffs
and International Trade

One of the most important tools of foreign economic policy is the tariff. Tariffs allow the country levying them to influence the pattern and volume of her trade with the outside world. By imposing different tariffs on different commodities, the country is able to change the relative prices of the commodities, which will result in a different trade pattern than would occur in the absence of the tariffs. In other words, the commodity composition of international trade will change. The country is also able to determine, within limits, the absolute volume of international trade. By increasing the tariff, the volume of international trade undertaken will generally fall. There will always be one tariff so prohibitively high that international trade will cease altogether. On the other hand, a decrease of the tariff rate will usually lead to a rise in trade volume. A negative tariff, or subsidy, may even lead to an expansion of international trade over and above the free trade volume.

1. Arguments for Protection

There are several noneconomic arguments which might make it desirable for a country to trade less, and to move to a position of greater autarky. The desire to preserve a certain way of life, isolated from foreign influences, may be so strong that a country is willing to pay a certain economic price for the attainment of this social objective. Greater self-sufficiency is often a military objective. The manufacture of arms and heavy industrial equipment as well as the production of agricultural commodities are examples of industries which can be important for national defense.

In all these cases the benefits to be derived from greater protection should

139

always be weighed against the additional costs incurred by the protective policy. Alternatives to protecting the industry against foreign competition must be considered, too. Stockpiling of the commodities deemed essential for the defense effort is one alternative. Other possibilities include the support of the armament industry by policies other than the restriction of foreign trade, such as tax advantages or outright subsidies.

Economic arguments for protection, in their attempt to justify the use of a tariff, invariably appeal to the divergence of private and social benefits and costs. Private and social benefits can diverge if certain benefits from the production process accrue to society as a whole, yet not to the entrepreneur, who is unable to charge an appropriate price—quite often because the relevant markets have not been formed or cannot be formed without undue costs. It is also possible that private and social costs are not identical. Producers may, for instance, be able to avoid paying certain costs by imposing them on other members of society.

The classical example of a divergence of social and private benefits and costs is the so-called *infant industry*. This term refers to a newly established industry which has not yet reached an output level allowing it to benefit from certain economies of scale expected to exist at higher output levels. A protective tariff would help such an industry to get off the ground and achieve levels of production at which the industry can be competitive in the world market. As soon as this competitive level is achieved, the tariff can be removed, and the industry is then forced to compete with the most efficient outside producers in order to ensure its own efficiency. Again, it is desirable to investigate alternative courses of action. A state-guaranteed loan, a tax advantage, or an outright subsidy may help the industry at a smaller cost to society as a whole than would a tariff. On the other hand, the amount of direct or indirect subsidy which the industry receives makes the costs incurred by society as a whole more apparent than they would be when a tariff is imposed, possibly inducing society to take a stand on whether or not the cost is worthwhile.

2. Effects of a Tariff

Several economic effects of a tariff deserve mentioning. It is important to realize that the imposition of a tariff on commodities imported from abroad[1] will affect not only the economy of the country imposing the tariff but will also have profound effects on her trading partners.

---

[1] In this discussion we will concentrate on tariffs levied on imports. It should be pointed out, however, that export tariffs are perfectly symmetrical to import tariffs in their economic effects.

a. Consumption, Production, Revenue, and Distribution Effects

The United States and the United Kingdom supply and demand curves for cloth are shown in Figure 9-1. In the absence of international trade, the price of cloth will be determined by the intersection of the supply and demand curves in each country. The price in the United States will be above the price in the United Kingdom. As soon as free international trade starts, one world price will be established for both countries together, excluding transport costs. If we recall that a necessary condition for the new world price to be an equilibrium price is that trade between the two countries must be balanced, we find that this condition is fulfilled in Figure 9-1, where the United States imports FI of cloth and the United Kingdom exports KN at the going world price $EO^{US}(=JO^{UK})$.

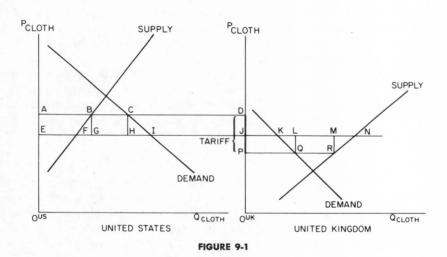

FIGURE 9-1

Now let us suppose that the United States imposes a tariff of the magnitude DP on her cloth imports from the United Kingdom.[2] As a result, the price of cloth in the United States increases to AO^{US}, and the price in the United Kingdom decreases to PO^{UK}. For the new prices to be equilibrium prices, the condition that exports equal imports must be fulfilled. Cloth imports of BC by the United States are matched by cloth exports of QR by the United Kingdom. Note that the tariff will affect the prices in both the United States and the United Kingdom.

---

[2] It is possible to substitute "an export tariff by the United Kingdom" at this juncture without affecting any of the following conclusions. This results from the symmetry between the effects of import and export tariffs already mentioned in the preceding footnote.

First of all, there is a *consumption effect* with respect to cloth. In the United States the consumption of cloth will decrease from EI to AC.[3] Decreased cloth consumption in the United States is due to the rise in price which follows directly from the imposition of the tariff. Second, there is a *production effect* of the tariff. The increased protection afforded the cloth industry in the United States leads to an expansion of output from EF to AB. Third, there is a *revenue effect* consisting of a change in government receipts because of the tariff. In our example there is initially a zero tariff, naturally bringing no revenue. Then a tariff of DP, multiplied by the quantity of imports after the imposition of the tariff, namely BC (=QR), gives the total amount of tariff revenue. The total government receipts are indicated by the sum of two areas, namely BCHG plus LMRQ. Finally, there is a *redistribution effect*, reflecting the fact that producers now receive a price for their commodities which is above their increase in production costs. This amount, ABFE, now accrues to producers in the form of economic rent, but it used to be part of the consumer's surplus which the residents derived because they were able to purchase the commodity at the low pretariff price, yet derived from it utility equal to the area under the demand curve.

It is clear that the magnitude of the effects described depends on the size of the tariff as well as on the elasticities of the supply and demand curves involved. This is easy to see when we change the shape of some of the curves in Figure 9-1 and observe the changes in the size of the areas discussed.

b. The Terms of Trade

Traditionally, the effects of a tariff on the terms of trade have been studied with great care, and they will occupy our attention for the remainder of this section. In Figure 9-1 we show that a tariff of the size DP increases the domestic price of the commodity by only a fraction of this amount, namely, AE, while simultaneously lowering the foreign price of the commodity by JP. Note that the United States is now able to buy the imports at the *lower* price PO^{UK} from the United Kingdom, but that the domestic price in the United States, after the duty has been collected by the United States government, is now at the higher level AO^{US}. The difference between the different prices can also be brought out in the traditional international trade offer curve diagram.

In Figure 9-2 we show the free trade offer curves of the United States and the United Kingdom, TOC^{US} and TOC^{UK} respectively. The free trade terms of trade, TOT, are determined by the intersection of the two countries' trade offer curves. If the United States imposes a 100 per cent tariff on the importation of cloth, and the tariff is levied in terms of wheat by the United

---

[3] This as well as the other effects discussed below have symmetrical counterparts in the United Kingdom which will operate in exactly the opposite direction.

States government, then the new offer curve TOC$_T^{US}$ will evolve. This offer curve, including the tariff, represents a displacement of the free trade offer curve TOC^{US} by the amount of the tariff, here shown as AB. Note that the tariff is an *ad valorem* tariff (here 100 per cent) on the value of the imports but is levied in terms of wheat. The tariff rate is given by t = AB/BC. The total tariff *revenue* (in terms of wheat) is equal to AB.

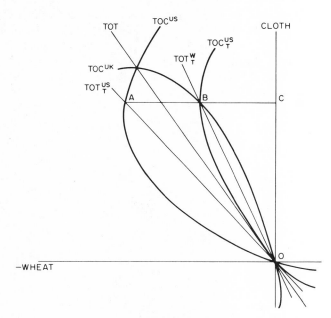

FIGURE 9-2

The intersection of the new trade offer curve TOC$_T^{US}$ and the British trade offer curve TOC^{UK} determines the new global terms of trade TOT$_T^{G}$. It now takes a smaller quantity of wheat to import the same quantity of cloth than it did before the tariff was imposed by the United States. This will be referred to as a "favorable" movement in the terms of trade for the United States. As seen from the viewpoint of the United States consumer or firm, however, the terms of trade have worsened because of the tariff. This is so because the domestic resident now faces a set of terms of trade which comprises not only the world market price for the commodity, but also the amount of the tariff. Thus the United States domestic term of trade would indicate that a greater quantity of exports is needed to obtain the same quantity of imports.

Compared with the free trade terms of trade, therefore, the external terms of trade which the United States faces in world markets have improved, while domestic terms of trade have deteriorated. It will be true that the free trade terms of trade will lie somewhere between the limits set by the domestic and global terms of trade, *including* the tariff. The precise position of the different terms of trade vis-à-vis each other is determined by the elasticities of the two countries' offer curves. The results of this analysis are consistent with the results obtained in the analysis of Figure 9-1, where the domestic price, including the tariff, increased in the United States while the world market price decreased.

The tariff could also be levied in terms of the import commodity, cloth. Under these circumstances the new offer curve for the United States, including the tariff, represents not a horizontal displacement of the free trade offer curve by the amount of the tariff, but a *vertical* displacement. This situation is shown in Figure 9-3, where the trade offer curve, including the tariff, TOC_T^{US}, is a vertical displacement of the free trade offer curve TOC^{US} by the amount of the tariff. This time the tariff *revenue* DE is collected in terms of cloth, and the tariff *rate* is DE/EF.

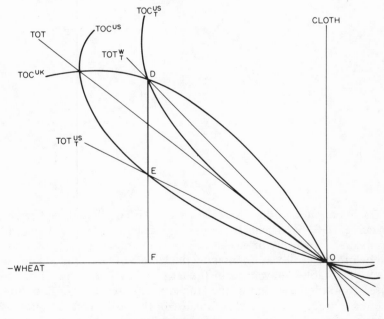

FIGURE 9-3

An important consideration is the use to which the collected tariff proceeds are put. If the government consumes the tariff proceeds itself, no further problems arise. If, on the other hand, the government wants to consume the other commodity, too, it has to enter the world market to obtain it. By doing this the government will add its own demand to the private demand for this commodity and new trade offer curves will be generated. The new trade offer curves will lead to different terms of trade, thereby inducing the private sector to rearrange its spending patterns to take account of the changing relative prices.

Similar complications will result from government redistribution of the proceeds collected from the tariff if the recipients of these government subsidies do not consume the subsidies directly but intend to consume a different commodity unit. In this case the changing private demand pattern will lead to the formation of new trade offer curves and, in turn, necessitate a readjustment of all equilibria.

It is apparent from the foregoing discussion that tariffs will have profound effects on the economic welfare of a country and of different economic groups within a country. A discussion of these welfare repercussions will be postponed until Section 9-4 below.

3. Tariff Policy

a. The Optimum Tariff

There exists a unique tariff which permits a country to reach the highest indifference curve attainable. The existence of such a tariff is due to two opposing forces which are at work as the height of the tariff is increased: (1) the terms of trade tend to turn more and more in favor of the country levying the tariff, while at the same time (2) the volume of imports tends to be more and more curtailed because of the higher tariff. An optimum position is reached when the gain due to (1) exceeds the loss from (2) by the greatest possible margin.

The country imposing the tariff, here the United States, wishes to reach the highest possible indifference curve. She knows that at any given terms of trade the United Kingdom is willing to trade any commodity combination represented by a point on her trade offer curve. The problem is to find the commodity combination which will fulfill both these conditions simultaneously. The desired commodity combination is the one at which one of the United States trade indifference curves is tangent to the British trade offer curve. The tangency position assures that there is no higher United States trade indifference curve than can be reached *given* the British trade offer curve. Such a point is shown by A in Figure 9-4.

Having determined the optimal commodity combination, all that is left for the United States to do is to levy a tariff which will bend her own trade offer curve in such a way that it will go through point A. The new United States trade offer curve, after the imposition of the tariff, is labeled TOC_T^{US}.

A further important point requires attention. The position of point A demarks the optimal trade combination for the United States. To offer her residents an inducement to trade precisely this commodity combination, namely, to export AB of wheat in exchange for BO of cloth imports, the price ratio confronting United States residents must be equal to the slope of a line which is tangent to the trade indifference curve TI_0^{US} at point A. This line, labeled AC, shows the domestic price ratio after the imposition of the tariff in the United States.

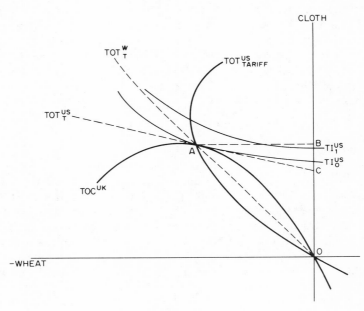

FIGURE 9-4

The world price ratio which will prevail after the United States has imposed the tariff is shown by the line AO in Figure 9-4. Clearly, the world price ratio and the United States *domestic* price ratio have to differ by the amount of duty collected on the commodities entering the United States. The world price ratio is AB/BO, and the domestic price ratio is AB/BC. The tariff rate, t (expressed in per cent), which will make the two price ratios equal, can be determined as follows:

$$(1 + t)AB/BO = AB/BC \qquad (9\text{-}1)$$

The tariff rate, t, can be derived by rewriting equation 9-1 as follows:

$$1 + t = \frac{AB/BC}{AB/BO} \quad \text{and}$$

$$t = \frac{BO}{BC} - 1 \qquad (9\text{-}2)$$

$\dfrac{BO}{BC}$ can be expanded by dividing numerator and denominator by OC:

$\dfrac{BO/OC}{BC/OC}$. We also know that BC = BO − OC. Thus we get

$$\frac{BO}{BC} = \frac{BO/OC}{BC/OC} = \frac{BO/OC}{(BO - OC)/OC} = \frac{BO/OC}{BO/OC - 1} \qquad (9\text{-}3)$$

From equation 5-2 we know that BO/OC is a measure of the price elasticity of the offer curve, i.e., BO/OC = ϵ. The expression in 9-3 reduces therefore to

$$\frac{BO}{BC} = \frac{\epsilon}{\epsilon - 1}$$

Inserting this into equation 9-2, we get:

$$t = \frac{\epsilon}{\epsilon - 1} - 1 = \frac{1}{\epsilon - 1} \qquad (9\text{-}5)$$

which is the optimum tariff formula desired.

A few properties of the optimum tariff formula may be mentioned here. If the elasticity of the foreign trade offer curve is infinity, then the optimum tariff $t = 1/(\epsilon - 1)$ will be equal to zero. A small country facing a *given* set of terms of trade and able to trade any quantity she desires at these terms of trade will find it to her advantage not to levy any tariff at all. On the other hand, if a country faces a unit elastic foreign trade offer curve, then she should levy a tariff which approaches infinity. In order to explain this seemingly unusual result, let us remind ourselves that a unit elastic foreign trade offer curve means that the other country is willing to give up a *fixed* quantity of exports in exchange for any quantity of imports. It would be to the advantage of any country to exploit this willingness to the greatest possible extent. The way to do this is to levy an extremely high tariff. Lastly, if the foreign trade offer curve has an elasticity smaller than one, the optimum tariff formula will yield a negative value. This can be taken as an indication that no optimal tariff exists when the foreign trade offer curve is inelastic. It will always be to the advantage of the country in question to move to somewhere in the elastic portion of the foreign trade offer curve, because she will thereby reach a higher trade indifference curve. This follows from the fact that the trade indifference curves in Figure 9-4 slope downward to the right and can therefore be tangent only to a foreign trade offer curve which also slopes downward and to the right. An inelastic foreign trade offer curve, however, slopes upward, and cannot be tangent to a downward sloping trade indifference curve.

When a country is able to impose a tariff she will always find it to her advantage to trade on a point located on the elastic portion of the other country's trade offer curve. The optimal tariff rate is equal to $1/(\epsilon - 1)$.

b. Retaliation

Let us suppose that the United States imposes an optimal tariff. She does this by modifying the original trade offer curve TOC_0^{US} shown in Figure 9-5 into TOC_1^{US}. At point B a United States trade indifference curve is tangent to United Kingdom's offer curve TOC_0^{UK}, and B denotes therefore the new point of equilibrium. Faced with the new United States trade offer curve TOC_1^{US}, the United Kingdom might now want to impose an optimal tariff herself. By following the same procedure of determining the point of tangency of a British trade indifference curve with the new United States trade offer curve, she is able to find the optimal tariff, and modifies her trade offer curve to TOC_1^{UK}. The new equilibrium point is marked C. At C the United Kingdom is on a higher trade indifference curve than she was at B.

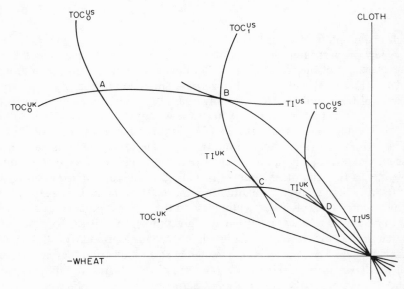

FIGURE 9-5

The procedure of retaliation and counter-retaliation can continue for many rounds. After the United States is faced with the new tariff-ridden British trade offer curve TOC_1^{UK}, she will want to take another look at her own tariff structure and revise it in the light of the British reaction. Given the shape of the curve as drawn in Figure 9-5, the United States will want to modify her tariff and reshape her trade offer curve into TOC_2^{US}. The new equilibrium is now D.

We note that the retaliatory tariff increases, and that each one, as an optimal countermove to the other country's tariff policy, will result in a smaller and smaller volume of international trade between the countries. The free trade volume of trade is given by the commodity bundle A. After the imposition of the initial United States tariff, the volume of trade is reduced to B, the British retaliation results in C, and the United States counter-retaliation pushes the trade volume down to D.

The question arises whether retaliation will continue until finally the volume of trade is reduced to zero. In order to answer this question, we recall that it is the position of one country's trade indifference curve in relation to the other country's trade offer curve which is decisive as far as the height of the optimum tariff is concerned. If the first country's trade indifference curve is tangent to the other country's trade offer curve at a point which already lies on the first country's trade offer curve, no further tariff could allow the first country to reach a higher trade indifference curve.

This case is illustrated by point D in Figure 9-5. The United States counter-retaliatory move resulted, as we saw, in the trade offer curve TOC_2^{US} and brought the volume of trade down to point D. Now we find that a British trade indifference curve, TI^{UK}, is already tangent to the United States trade offer curve at this point. No further tariff imposed by the United Kingdom will allow her to reach a higher trade indifference curve, and the United Kingdom, therefore, has no incentive to modify her trade offer curve TOC_1^{UK} any further. If the United Kingdom does not change her existing tariff structure, the United States has no incentive to modify her tariffs either. Point D will be the final point of equilibrium, and no further retaliatory tariffs are to be expected.

c. Tariff Cycles

Trade indifference curves and trade offer curves may have a peculiar constellation which will lead to the emergence of tariff cycles. Tariff cycles may be described as situations in which both countries will alternate between high and low tariffs.

Consider Figure 9-6. TOC_1^{US} and TOC_1^{UK} show the initial situation where both the United States and the United Kingdom have a small tariff placed on their imports. The United States will find it to her advantage to move from point A to point B by imposing an optimal tariff, which will change her trade offer curve to TOC_2^{US}. Faced with this new trade offer curve, the United Kingdom will want to impose an optimal tariff herself, changing her trade offer curve to TOC_2^{UK}, reaching the new equilibrium point C. Now the United States will reconsider her previous move, and since one of her own trade indifference curves is tangent to Britain's new trade offer curve TOC_2^{UK} at point D, which lies in the *old* United States trade offer curve TOC_1^{US}, the United States will return to her *old* tariff. Now it is Britain's turn to reconsider the situation, and since one of her trade indifference curves is

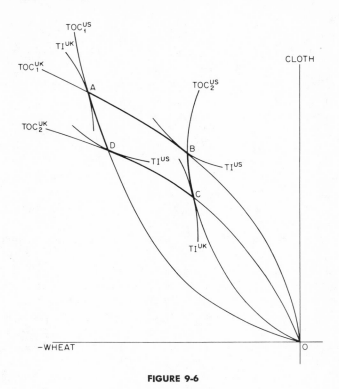

FIGURE 9-6

tangent to the United States TOC_1^{US} trade offer curve at point A, she will also want to return to her old tariff level, and trade along offer curve TOC_1^{UK}. This means a return to point A, at which the United States will again find it advantageous to levy a tariff, leading to point B again, and a new round in the tariff cycle will start.

4. Welfare Effects of a Tariff

Next we will consider the welfare implications of imposing a tariff. It is clear that a country will impose a tariff only if it will make her in some sense better off. The movement to a higher trade indifference curve referred to earlier represents an improvement in welfare for the country under consideration. The imposition of an optimal tariff makes the country as well off as she can be. It is also clear that the other country will experience a decrease in her welfare due to the fact that she will wind up on a lower trade indifference curve. Furthermore, there is the possibility that retaliatory actions taken by the two countries will lead to an ultimate decrease in the welfare of both countries involved, despite the fact that at each successive step in the retaliatory process the country imposing the tariff will gain slightly.

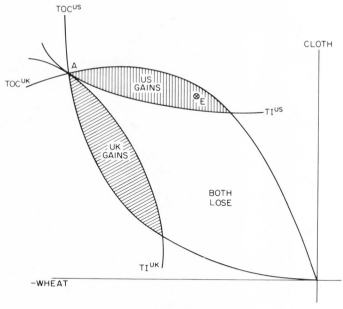

FIGURE 9-7

The final welfare gains and losses will depend on the position of the final equilibrium that obtains. Let us say that the initial no-tariff situation is represented by point A in Figure 9-7. If the final equilibrium point is a point like E, located in the region bordered by the United Kingdom's trade offer curve and the United States' trade indifference curve through A, the United States will gain. This follows from the fact that any point which is located on a trade indifference curve higher than TI^{US} represents a potentially superior welfare position for the United States. Plainly, the United Kingdom is worse off as a result, since any final equilibrium point to the right of her trade indifference curve TI^{UK} represents a lower level of welfare.

Similarly, a final equilibrium point in the region bounded by the United States trade offer curve and the British trade indifference curve will denote a higher level of welfare for the United Kingdom and a lower one for the United States. Lastly, both countries may wind up on a trade indifference curve which is lower than the free trade indifference curve through point A and, as a consequence, both countries would lose due to the tariff measures taken. A joint effort to remove the tariffs will then lead to an increase in welfare for both countries.

The dilemma facing countries contemplating the imposition of tariffs is that quite often the incentive system is such that for one country alone it will be beneficial to impose a tariff, but for both countries together it will be better to refrain from the imposition of a tariff. The problem appears to be one of setting up appropriate machinery which will either remove the incentive for a single country to impose a tariff or else distribute the gains to be derived from mutual tariff removal in a suitable fashion.

a. The Trade Possibility Curve and a Country's Welfare[4]

In discussing the free trade opportunities of a large country, the *trade possibilities curve* was introduced to show the commodity combinations attainable by a country engaging in international trade. The same tool may be utilized to show the trade possibilities open to a large country imposing a tariff. The case of a small country facing a given set of terms of trade becomes redundant in connection with the imposition of tariffs, since the optimal tariff a small country should levy is zero, as was shown in Section 9-3-a above. Thus we will deal only with the large country case in the subsequent discussion of the effects of a tariff.

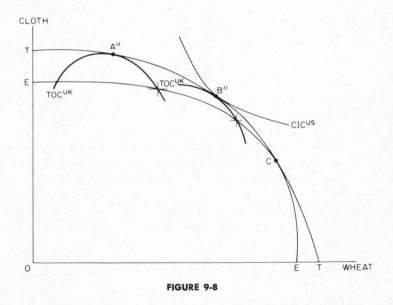

FIGURE 9-8

The trade possibilities curve is derived in a similar fashion as in Section 8-2-b. That is, the origin of the foreign (United Kingdom) country's coordinate system is moved along the production possibility curve of the large country (United States). This is done in Figure 9-8. If the United States is able to impose a tariff, she can trade *any* commodity combination she desires, provided she chooses a point located on United Kingdom's trade

---

[4] This section, up to page 153, may be skipped without affecting continuity.

offer curve. Thus, by levying the appropriate tariff, the United Kingdom can be made to exchange the desired commodity combination. By slowly shifting the United Kingdom's trade offer curve along the production possibility curve of the United States, we can trace the collection of maximum commodity combinations that the United Kingdom is willing to trade. Points A'', B'', and C in Figure 9-8 are points which can be reached in the manner described. The collection of these points has been described as an "envelope" of all possible British trade offer curves. The envelope describing the United States trade possibility curve, allowing for the imposition of a tariff, is labeled TT.

By comparing Figure 9-8 to Figure 8-4, which depicted the trade possibility curve in the free trade (no-tariff) situation, we can immediately see that the trade possibility curve for the tariff case (TT) will always be located outside the trade possibility curve for the free trade case (EE in Figure 8-4). The actual commodity combination the United States chooses to trade with the United Kingdom is determined by the point at which the highest possible United States community indifference curve is tangent to the envelope trade possibility curve. Such a point is labeled B'' in Figure 9-8. Evidently, a point such as B'' in Figure 9-8, which lies on a higher trade possibility curve than the points on the trade possibilities curve for the free trade case, will allow the country to attain a superior commodity combination.

By imposing an optimal tariff, it is always possible for a country to reach a commodity combination that is potentially superior to the free trade situation.

Two *caveats* are in order. First, there is always the possibility of retaliation by other countries, which could possibly make the country worse off than she would have been under free trade. The different possibilities for gain or loss in the two-country case with retaliation have already been discussed. Secondly, there is the possibility that the commodity bundle which is attained by restricted trade contains less of one commodity than the free trade bundle. The question of income distribution then looms over our heads. Suffice it here to point out that there is always one commodity combination that could be reached by subsequent trade which will be superior in the sense that it actually contains more of both commodities than the free trade situation. Thus there is always the potential for an unambiguous welfare increase.

b. The Welfare of an Economic Group

Hitherto we concentrated on the welfare of the country as a whole and neglected any complications that might arise due to changing patterns of income distribution. Again we refer to the extensive discussion of this problem in Section 8-3 of the preceding chapter. There, international trade was shown to lead to a reallocation of factors of production between different uses, and assurance of continued employment of all available resources required the real wage of the factor of production intensive in the expanding industry to rise, while the wage of the factor of production intensive in the contracting industry declines.

This analysis can be applied conveniently to the changes which are brought about by the introduction of a tariff. Imposition of a tariff will tend to increase the domestic production of the protected commodity, while the production of the unprotected commodity will decrease. Consequently, the factor of production which is used intensively in the contracting industry will have to accept a lower wage if it is to find employment in the expanding industry. Only if the factor is willing to accept a lower wage will factor intensities in production be changed so that more of this factor will be used in the expanding (tariff-protected) industry.

The reader is referred to Section 8-3 for a complete discussion of the relevant arguments, especially proof that the *absolute* wage received by the factor intensive in the contracting industry will decrease.

The imposition of a tariff will improve the welfare of the factor used intensively in the protected industry, while lowering the welfare of the other factor.

5. The Effective Protective Tariff Rate

In the previous discussion it was implicitly assumed that we produce the final commodities directly from the original factors of production. The imposed tariff was analyzed as far as its effect on prices of the protected commodities was concerned.

Most commodities, however, are *not* produced directly from the original factors of production, but utilize intermediate products as inputs. The automotive industry, for instance, uses products manufactured by the tire, paint, steel, glass, and many other industries as inputs for automobile production. It would be of great interest to find out how much protection is afforded to the United States automotive industry if we impose a tariff on imported automobiles. In other words, we are asking how much protection is afforded to the automobile production process itself. The amount of protection given to an industry by a tariff is called the *effective protective tariff rate*. The effective protective rate for the industry under consideration shows by how much the value added in this industry can exceed the value added in the absence of tariff protection.

The protection afforded to the automotive industry will depend on how high a tariff is levied not only on its products, but also on its inputs. If, for instance, all automobile parts can enter the country at a low duty while automobiles are protected by a high duty, the result will be a very high effective protective rate for the automobile-assembling firms in the United States. Conversely, if inputs can enter the United States only under a very high duty and the final product is not at all (or very little) protected, then United States assembly plants will be faced with higher than world market prices for their inputs, yet must compete in the automobile market against foreign manufacturers. The effective protective rate for the automobile-assembling process is in this case very low, and can, indeed, become negative.

Formally, we can state that the effective protective rate of the industry a (epr$_a$) is equal to the nominal tariff rate (t$_a$) on industry a's products, minus the weighted tariff rate on the industry's inputs (Σw t$_k$) divided by the value added per dollar of output (v$_a$) in the industry under consideration. Where w is the dollar value of the input k per dollar value of the product a, i.e., the share which this particular factor contributes to the cost of the output, and t$_k$ is the tariff levied on this input. We can write:

$$\text{epr}_a = \frac{t_a - \Sigma w\, t_k}{v_a} = \frac{\text{tariff rate on product} - \text{average tariff on inputs}}{\text{value added per dollar of output}} \quad (9\text{-}6)$$

The effective protective rate increases as the tariff rate on the output a increases. It decreases as the tariff rates on the inputs k increase. If the weighted average tariff on the inputs exceeds the tariff on the output, the effective protective rate on the value added in the industry a will become negative.

This rate is very important for the assessment of the protection afforded to individual industries of a country. Even without changing the tariff levied on the output of an industry, the effective protection can change if the tariff on the direct inputs changes. Not only the tariff on the final product is decisive, but the whole tariff *structure* plays a role in determining the protection afforded to an industry. It should be noted, however, that only the tariffs levied on the direct inputs to a production process are important. The tariffs levied on inputs used to produce the direct inputs used in the production process are irrelevant for our consideration. Thus the tariff rate on iron ore, which is used to produce the steel for automobile production, is irrelevant for the determination of the effective protective tariff rate of the automotive industry. Only the tariffs on the direct inputs, like steel, and the product, automobiles, are of importance.

6. Empirical Evidence

Empirical evidence assessing the effects of the removal or imposition of tariffs will be presented in Chapter 10 in connection with the discussion of the welfare gains and losses due to the formation of a customs union. Here we will restrict ourselves to the presentation of data calculating effective protective tariff rates.

Two of the pioneering empirical studies were undertaken by Bela Balassa[5] and Giorgio Basevi.[6] Both these studies point out that the nominal tariff rate is misleading in that it leaves out the effect of tariffs imposed on raw materials or intermediate products. It turns out that the effective protective rate is often quite different from the nominal tariff rate, which does not take this into account. Thus traditional nominal tariff rates do not give an accurate picture of the extent of protection afforded any given industry or of the height of the average tariff of a country.

A few selected nominal and effective protective rates for United States industries (1962) and average rates for a group of industrialized countries are given in Tables 9-1 and 9-2.

TABLE 9-1

1962 Tariff Rates on U. S. Imports

Commodity	Nominal	Effective
Wood Products	12.8	26.4
Ingots and Steel Forms	10.6	106.7
Automobiles	6.8	5.1
Airplanes	9.2	8.8
Ships	5.5	2.1
Paper & Paper Products	3.1	0.7
Rolling Mill Products	7.1	−2.2
Agricultural Machinery	.4	−6.9

Source: B. Balassa, "Tariff Protection in Industrial Countries: An Evaluation," *Journal of Political Economy* (The University of Chicago Press, December 1965), p. 580. By permission of the author and publisher.

TABLE 9-2

1962 Overall Weighted Tariff Averages

Country	Nominal	Effective
United States	11.6	20.0
United Kingdom	15.5	27.8
Common Market	11.9	18.6
Sweden	6.8	12.5
Japan	16.2	29.5

Source: B. Balassa, op. cit., p. 588.

[5] B. Balassa, "Tariff Protection in Industrial Countries: An Evaluation," *Journal of Political Economy*, December 1965.

[6] G. Basevi, "The United States Tariff Structure: Estimates of Effective Rates of Protection of U. S. Industries and Industrial Labor," *Review of Economics and Statistics*, May 1966.

Two observations need to be made: For one, the knowledge of nominal tariff rates yields no clue to the height of the effective tariff protection afforded an industry. In the United States we find examples where the effective rate is more than ten times the nominal rate. In other industries the nominal rate and the effective rate are virtually identical. Without doubt, the most interesting cases arise when the effective rate is actually negative. We will recall from the previous section that this result occurs if the weighted average of the tariffs on the inputs used in the production process is greater than the tariff on the output. The effective protective rate on the value added by this industry therefore becomes negative.

Secondly, the cross-country data indicate that effective tariff rates for the countries studied are almost twice as high as the nominal rates. International comparisons of tariff rates have to be undertaken with care.

SUGGESTED FURTHER READINGS

Balassa, Bela, "Tariff Protection in Industrial Countries," *Journal of Political Economy*, December 1965.

Basevi, Giorgio, "The United States Tariff Structure: Estimates of Effective Rates of Protection of United States Industries and Industrial Labor," *Review of Economics and Statistics*, May 1966.

Haberler, Gottfried, "A Survey of International Trade Theory," *Special Papers in International Economics*, No. 1, International Finance Section, Princeton University, 1961, Chapter 6.

————, *The Theory of International Trade*. London: Hodge, 1936, Chapters 13–16.

Johnson, Harry, *International Trade and Economic Growth*. London: Allen & Unwin, 1958, Chapter 2.

Vanek, Jaroslav, *International Trade: Theory and Economic Policy*. Homewood, Ill.: Richard D. Irwin, 1962, Chapter 16.

CHAPTER 10

Economic Unions
and International Trade

The theory of tariffs surveyed in the last chapter constitutes an example of a discriminatory trade policy which is applied uniformly to all countries. But not always will countries want to discriminate equally against all other countries. There are several possible forms of organization which allow countries to discriminate only against a select group of countries. Most prominent among these are free trade areas, customs unions, and common markets. The main difference between these three principal ways of organizing a preferential trade area lies in the degree of interdependence achieved by the member countries.

A *free trade area* consists of a group of countries which have abolished all tariff barriers between themselves but maintain their individual tariffs vis-à-vis the outside world. An important problem arises in the implementation of the free trade area concept since commodities imported from the outside world tend to enter the free trade area via the country with the lowest external tariff. The policing problem is made somewhat easier if the countries forming the free trade area do not have any joint boundaries, thus making the transfer of commodities inside the area easier to control. A good example which fulfills this condition is the European Free Trade Area (EFTA), which consists of the "Outer Seven": Austria, Denmark, Norway, Portugal, Sweden, Switzerland, and the United Kingdom.

A *customs union* differs from a free trade area in that it has a common external tariff which applies to the imports of any member country from the outside world. Free movement of all products is assured within the union, and thus the problem of intra-union trade of imported commodities no longer exists.

Finally, a *common market* not only allows for the free movement of products, like the free trade area and the customs union, but permits in addition the free movement of all factors of production. Thus the common market represents the most complete concept of economic integration among the three. The European Economic Community, comprising Belgium, France, Germany, Italy, Luxembourg, and the Netherlands, now has a complete customs union and is working toward implementation of the common market goal.

In this chapter we will focus attention on the economics of the customs union. The analysis of the customs union can easily be extended to cover the cases of the free trade area and the common market also.

1. Effects of a Customs Union

The formation of a customs union involves the changing of tariff patterns between the countries forming the union as well as between the union members and the outside world. We will analyze the effects of the tariff changes on trade volume and prices and will also try to indicate what changes in economic welfare may be expected in light of the policies pursued. Of special interest is the question of whether total welfare will be increased or decreased due to the formation of the customs union.

In our analysis we will assume that there are only three countries: the United Kingdom, France, and the Netherlands. France and the Netherlands will be the two countries which are forming the customs union, and the United Kingdom will represent the "outsider." Let us assume, too, that the Dutch supply and demand curves for cloth, S^N and D^N, are as indicated in Figure 10-1, and that cloth can be produced in both France and the United Kingdom under constant cost conditions. The supply curves for these two countries are labeled S^F and S^{UK}. The relevant prices of cloth (in terms of wheat) are also given in Table 10-1. The Dutch tariff vis-à-vis the outside world is assumed to be 50 per cent.

TABLE 10-1

	Producer Country	
	France	United Kingdom
Cloth Price (in terms of wheat)	100	80
Tariff (50 per cent)	50	40
Price including tariff	150	120

Before formation of the customs union between France and the Netherlands, we have the following situation: in the absence of any imports, the

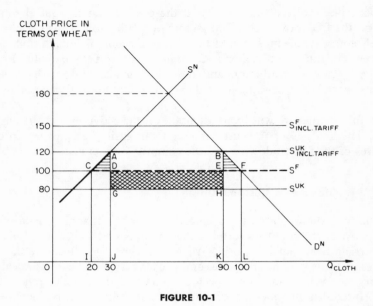

FIGURE 10-1

price for cloth in the Netherlands is 180 units of wheat. This price is indicated by the intersection of the Dutch supply and demand curves for cloth. But the price of cloth would never rise to this level in the Netherlands, because before the formation of the customs union Dutchmen could always buy cloth from the least costly outside producer, here the United Kingdom, and after paying the tariff would be able to obtain each piece of cloth for 120 units.

Dutch producers will supply 30 bales of cloth because up to this quantity they are able to supply the markets at a price below 120 units, and any remaining quantity, here an additional 60 bales, would be imported from the United Kingdom. The effective supply curve before the formation of the customs union is therefore the heavy line in Figure 10-1.

a. Trade Creation

After the Netherlands and France form the customs union, all tariffs between these two countries are abolished, while the tariff toward outsiders remains at, let us say, the customary 50 per cent. It is now possible for Dutch residents to buy their cloth in France for 100 units, 20 units cheaper than the British price, which still includes the tariff charge.

The result of this cheapening of the imported cloth is that larger quantities of cloth will be imported. The Dutch cloth industry will cut back production to 20 bales, and Dutch residents will buy an additional 80 bales of cloth from France. Imports have thereby increased from 60 to 80 bales.

The increase in imports is the result of a movement to a position of freer trade than prevailed prior to the abolition of the French-Dutch tariff. We will refer to this expansion of trade between countries as the *trade-creating effect* of a customs union. The total trade-creation effect can be subdivided into one due to production and another due to consumption.

The trade creation due to production takes place because before the formation of the union the British price for cloth, including the tariff, was 120 units, and Dutch manufacturers could produce up to 30 bales (point A on the supply curve) more cheaply than this. After foreign cloth becomes available to the Dutch at the price of 100 units, Dutch manufacturers can produce only 20 bales cheaper than this (point C on the supply curve). Consequently, the quantity CD (equal to 10 bales) will be supplied by foreign sources, leading to greater international trade, hence trade creation.

There is a welfare gain for Dutch residents involved in this process. The resource cost of producing the quantity CD of cloth is equal to the area under the Dutch supply curve,[1] AJIC. When the 10 bales of cloth are imported from France instead of being produced at home, Dutch residents have to pay only 100 units per bale. The total cost to the Netherlands is DJIC. The difference between the costs to Dutch producers and the import cost constitutes a net saving to Dutch residents equal to the shaded triangle ADC. This net saving can be interpreted as an increase in economic welfare due to the trade-creating effects of the customs union.

Similar to the welfare gains resulting from the saving in procurement cost, there is a welfare gain on the consumption side due to trade creation. Consumption of cloth in the Netherlands expands from 90 to 100 bales with the lowering of the cloth price pursuant to the formation of the customs union. The total utility derived by Dutch residents from the additional cloth can be approximated by the area under the demand curve,[2] BFLK. But the Dutch have to pay an amount equal to only FLKE for the additional 10 bales of cloth and experience a welfare gain equal to the shaded triangle BFE.

The total welfare gains from trade creation taking place after the formation of the customs union are the result of production and consumption effects. The magnitude of these welfare effects depends mainly on the following variables: (1) the height of the pre-union tariff, (2) the slope of the supply curve, and (3) the slope of the demand curve. If the pre-union tariff is higher, the welfare gains from the abolition of the tariff tend to be higher. In the figure we can see this as an initially greater spread between

[1] To establish this point one has to assume that the Dutch cloth industry is perfectly competitive. For the point that the area under the supply curve equals the cost of production, see any elementary textbook, e.g., P. A. Samuelson, *Economics*, 6th ed., McGraw-Hill, Chapter 22.
[2] This holds true if money can serve as an accurate measuring rod of utility derived. See any elementary textbook, such as Samuelson, *op. cit.*, p. 435, on this point.

the supply price of the United Kingdom, including the tariff, and the supply price of France. The triangles ADC and BFE showing the welfare gains will also be larger if the Dutch supply and demand curves are flatter, i.e., less steep. To establish this point we have to remember that the spread between the British and French supply curves is given, thus fixing the distances AD and BE. The flatter the Dutch supply and demand curves, the greater will be the distances CD and EF, and the greater the area of the triangles.

b. Trade Diversion

A customs union may succeed in securing the whole union market for the partner country. Quite often, however, it may be true that the partner country is not the world's most efficient producer of the product. This is the case in the example studied here, where the United Kingdom is the lowest cost producer. Only because France is within the union and the United Kingdom's products are discriminated against by a tariff is it possible for France to secure the union market.

After the formation of the union, the Netherlands no longer buys from the most efficient producer in the *world* but merely from the most efficient producer within the union, in this case France. The consequence of this is *trade diversion* from the low cost producer to the high cost producer.

Instead of importing 60 bales of cloth (in Figure 10-1 equal to AB, DE, or GH) from the United Kingdom, the Dutch will import 80 bales of cloth from France. We saw earlier that the 20 additional bales of cloth imports are due to trade creation, the welfare effects of which were analyzed at that time. Here we will focus attention on the 60 bales which were formerly imported from the United Kingdom and are now imported from France.

When importing the 60 bales of cloth from the United Kingdom, Dutch importers paid a price of 80 units of wheat per bale of cloth to the British exporter. Total payments were equal to the area GHKJ. Dutch consumers had to pay in addition a 50 per cent tariff (equal to the area ABHG), which made the total payments equal to the area ABKJ. But note that of these total payments by Dutch consumers, the tariff proceeds went to Dutch customs collectors, thus representing simply an income redistribution within the Netherlands. Crucial for our purposes is that Dutch residents had to pay to the foreign source, the United Kingdom, a total of GHKJ.

After the formation of the customs union, Dutch residents have to pay to French exporters an amount equal to DEKJ for the same quantity of cloth. Thus payments for product have increased by the amount DEHG, which is shown as the crosshatched area in the figure. Cloth is no longer supplied by the world's most efficient producer, but rather by the most efficient producer within the union.

As the formation of the union is responsible for the shifting from the lowest cost producer in the world to the lowest cost producer within the union, we can say that there will be welfare losses due to the trade-diverting effects of the customs union. The magnitude of the losses is shown by the size of the rectangle DEHG.

The net welfare effect of an economic union is the difference between its trade-creating and trade-diverting effects.

The preceding analysis can be extended to the case of foreign supply curves that are less than perfectly elastic. In this more general case the tariff is no longer borne exclusively by the importing country, but falls partially on the exporting country. The welfare gains and losses can no longer be assessed by comparing simple triangles and rectangles, and the geometry becomes somewhat involved.[3]

The policy implications of our analysis of customs union formation so far are fairly clear: while it is possible that the welfare gains due to trade creation are larger than the welfare losses due to trade diversion, it is also possible that the reverse holds true. Thus the formation of a customs union will not always lead unambiguously to an improvement in economic welfare. This fact is clearly attested to by the observable behavior of countries. Some countries try to form customs unions because the expected gains are larger than the expected losses, while others refrain from doing so for the opposite reasons.

2. Equilibrium Prices and Quantities

In most cases we cannot assume that one of the union partners is so small in relation to the other countries that her actions have no influence on the price at which the other countries are willing to buy and sell the commodities under consideration. To analyze the effects of a customs union on prices and quantities in all countries involved is our next task.

In Figure 10-2 we show the supply and demand curves for cloth for each one of the three countries, France, the Netherlands, and the United Kingdom. Again it will be assumed that France and the Netherlands are the two countries forming the union.

The pre-union situation is indicated by the heavy lines. The Netherlands is assumed to impose a 50 per cent tariff on cloth, while France imposes a 20 per cent tariff. Again, the outsider, the United Kingdom, is assumed to be the low cost producer. The equilibrium prices and quantities exported and imported are given in Table 10-2. Note that the domestic price in the United Kingdom is equal to the price paid by the importers of British cloth.

---

[3] The interested reader is referred to the appendix of Harry Johnson's article on "The Economic Theory of Customs Unions," in *Money, Trade, and Economic Growth*, Harvard, 1962.

The domestic prices in the Netherlands and France differ from the British price by the amount of the tariff. The Netherlands imports 30 bales of cloth to supplement her domestic production, France imports 20 bales, and, consequently, the United Kingdom exports 50 bales.

TABLE 10-2

	Netherlands	France	United Kingdom
Pre-Union			
Tariff	50%	20%	
Price	150	120	100
Exports (−) or Imports (+)	+30	+20	−50
Post Union			
Tariff	40%	40%	
Price	140	140	100
Exports (−) or Imports (+)	+60	−10	−50

When the Netherlands and France form the customs union, they abolish all internal tariffs and adopt a common external tariff which lies, let us say, between the limits set by the pre-union tariffs of 50 and 20 per cent. Let us assume that the external tariff fixed by the union members is 40 per cent.

We will turn first to the price determination in the union. First, we observe that there is now a common price for cloth in France and the Nether-

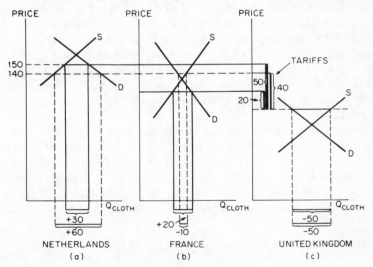

FIGURE 10-2 (a), (b), and (c)

lands because commodities are free to move from one country to the other without encountering any tariff obstacles. We can now say that the union price for cloth cannot be as high as the pre-union price for cloth in the Netherlands because, if it were actually *equal* to the old price, the following would hold true: (1) the Netherlands would want to import the same quantity as before because the price has not changed; (2) France would want to import less because the price has risen; and (3) the United Kingdom would want to export more, given that the price inside the union is equal to the old Dutch price, but the lower tariff which is now in existence means higher receipts for the United Kingdom, thus making exports more profitable. Obviously, (1), (2), and (3) cannot all hold true at the same time, because world exports would be greater than world imports. Thus it must be true that the pre-union price for cloth in the Netherlands represents an upper boundary which will prevail inside the union after its formation.

A similar argument can be made to show that in France the union price is no lower than the pre-union price for cloth.

The price for cloth in the United Kingdom may be higher, lower, or equal to the pre-union price. In the numerical and diagrammatical example provided, the British price is shown to be the same both before and after the formation of the Dutch-French customs union. In this case we will find that the volume of British trade with the union countries has remained unchanged. This is made possible because Dutch imports increased in the same amount (30 bales) that French purchases from abroad decreased. (Note that the decrease of French purchases is really made up of a genuine decrease in French imports from 20 to zero, and an increase in its exports by 10, providing a net change of 30.)

If Dutch imports had increased *more* than France's decreased, the net result would have been increased imports by the union countries, meaning a higher price and greater quantity of British exports. Conversely, had Dutch imports increased *less* than France's decreased, the union countries' imports would have shown a net reduction, resulting in a lower price and export quantity for the United Kingdom.

3. General Equilibrium Analysis

The analysis of the previous section can be extended to the two-commodity case with the help of the general equilibrium model developed in the first chapters of this book. The quantities which the union members are willing to exchange with outsiders, say, the United Kingdom, can be summarized in an *excess trade offer curve*, which shows the different cloth/wheat combinations that the union is willing to trade with the United Kingdom at different terms of trade. To derive this curve for the union partners, we con-

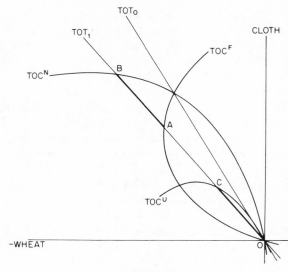

FIGURE 10-3

struct first the customary international trade offer curves for the union members: France (TOC^F in Figure 10-3) and the Netherlands (TOC^N). Then we determine the net quantities of the commodities which the partners are willing to trade with the outsider (United Kingdom) at all possible terms of trade. At the terms of trade TOT_0 trade between France and the Netherlands is balanced, and the union will not want to trade with the United Kingdom, resulting in a point on the excess trade offer curve which coincides with the origin. At different terms of trade, such as TOT_1, France will want to exchange quantities of cloth and wheat shown by OA, while the Netherlands will want to trade the larger quantities OB. As a result we find that there is an excess demand for wheat and an excess supply of cloth at the going prices. The union partners will wish to import wheat in exchange for cloth, as shown by the distance AB. This is the "excess offer" of cloth for wheat by the union, and it can be shown separately as the distance OC. The collection of all possible excess offers at different terms of trade generates the union's excess trade offer curve TOC^U.

The union's excess trade offer curve TOC^U and the trade offer curve of the outsider, TOC^{UK}, together determine the international terms of trade. In Figure 10-4 we show the trade offer curves and the equilibrium international terms of trade TOT_2. At these terms of trade there will be no excess demands or supplies of the two commodities in the world market.

The union's excess offer curve must now be modified to take account of any tariffs which the union may levy against imports from the outside country. This is shown in Figure 10-4 by the excess trade offer curve TOC^U_T. This curve,

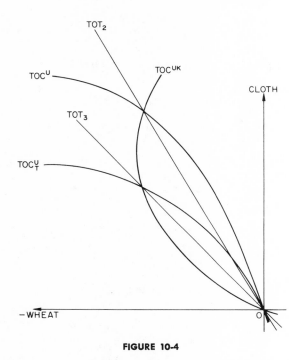

FIGURE 10-4

including the tariff, is derived by the customary method of displacing the original trade offer curve by the amount of the tariff levied upon the commodities. The external union tariff establishes the new terms of trade TOT_3, which are more favorable to the union. In most circumstances the volume of trade will be smaller than in the no-tariff situation. However, all the qualifications discussed in the chapter on the effects of tariffs apply also here. The theory of the optimal tariff can be applied to the customs union tariff, too. The union should levy an external tariff which will allow her to reach the highest possible trade indifference curve, given the position of the outsider's trade offer curve.

The question remains: Are the union partners better or worse off after forming their union and adopting the common external tariff? Figure 10-5 shows that the answer to this question cannot be given on a priori grounds alone. It all depends on the position of the excess offer curve for France and the Netherlands before (TOC^{F+N}) and after (TOC_T^U) the formation of the union. The excess trade offer curves before the formation of the union may lead to terms of trade which are more (TOC_0^{F+N}) or less (TOC_1^{F+N}) favorable than the union terms of trade (TOC_T^U). But we should not forget that not only are the terms of trade important in the determination of welfare gains and losses, but other factors enter as well. The final determination concerning the

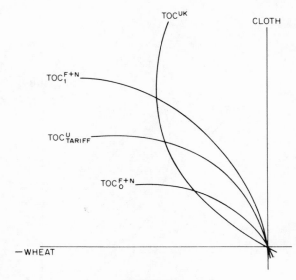

FIGURE 10-5

welfare effects of the union depends on which situation will allow the countries to reach the highest possible trade indifference curve.

Thus it is clear that the effects of the formation of a customs union on the member's trade with the outside world cannot be predicted with accuracy on a priori grounds. The theory of customs unions represents a good example of the fact that as soon as we move away from our simple two-country, two-commodity models, there is very little which can be said about possible price and quantity effects due to any change in economic policy.

4. Other Factors

There are other factors which may influence the decision calculus of countries considering forming a customs union. Among the more important economic reasons we find greater efficiency due to greater specialization within the union. The size of the market is enlarged considerably and, with it, the opportunities for large-scale production and distribution methods. At the same time, existing monopolies may be faced with more intensive foreign competition by producers located in the partner countries. Also, established firms with a secure market will suddenly have to defend their market position against the new competition. Enforced efficiency in the industries concerned can be an important by-product of the customs union formation.

A final word needs to be said about the *type* of countries most likely to experience large gains from the formation of a customs union. If the countries forming such a union are initially similar, the gains will tend to be larger than if the countries are initially dissimilar. The latter are already specialized to a large extent in the commodities in which they enjoy a comparative advantage. The additional gains to be expected from formation of a union and consequent elimination of tariff barriers are produced largely by the gains from exchange discussed earlier.[4] If, however, the countries are initially similar, then potential gains from specialization pursuant to the formation of the customs union also exist. The total anticipated gains are therefore larger.

Also, the greater the *size* of the customs union, the greater the gains will tend to be. We saw in our initial discussion that any customs union combines elements of freer trade within the union and protection of the union market vis-à-vis the outside world. The larger the union, the greater is the chance that the world's lowest cost producer is a union member, and that therefore all union members are afforded the advantage of being able to buy from the low cost producer. In other words, the chance of trade diversion playing an important role decreases as the size of the union increases. Finally, in the limiting case where the union encompasses the whole world, trade diversion is no longer possible, and only gains from trade creation are being reaped— which are now identical with the regular gains from trade due to the introduction of a free trade policy discussed in the first half of this book.

In addition to the economic reasons discussed, there may be others, especially of a political nature, which might influence the decision of a country to join or not to join a customs union or, perhaps, to bar certain prospective members from joining an already existing union. To enumerate all possible political implications of a customs union would, however, be considerably beyond the scope of this chapter.

5. Empirical Evidence

In this section we will limit ourselves to (1) an assessment of the trade-creating and trade-diverting effects of the European Economic Community, and (2) the probable magnitude of increased efficiency in resource use which can be expected as a result of the abolition of the tariffs between the union partners. By following this procedure we neglect all possible dynamic effects of the union formation. It has been argued that these dynamic effects are very important and probably of considerable magnitude. But reliable empirical evidence does not exist, and following our usual procedure we will limit ourselves to actual attempts of quantification.

The most comprehensive attempt to measure the trade-creating and trade-diverting effects of the European Economic Community has been undertaken

[4] See Section 8-2-a for the concepts of gains from exchange and gains from specialization.

by Bela Balassa.[5] The crucial assumption of Balassa's study is that the income elasticities of demand would have remained unchanged in the absence of the formation of the union. If we should observe, therefore, that the ex-post income elasticity of demand for imports (from partner countries *or* all countries combined) actually increased, we may take this as an indication that trade creation occurred. If, on the other hand, the income elasticity of demand for imports from nonmember countries declines, we can take this as evidence of the trade-diverting effects of the union.

Using aggregate data, Balassa finds some evidence of trade creation and no indication of trade-diverting effects. But disaggregation of the data shows that individual commodity classes experienced both trade creation and trade diversion. Trade creation was evident in fuels (where we see the effects of the EEC policy of shifting from expensive union sources to cheaper outside energy supplies), chemicals, machinery, and transportation equipment. Trade diversion occurred in the food sector (evidence of the protectionistic agricultural policy of the EEC), as well as in beverages, tobacco, raw materials, semi-manufactured commodities, and consumer durables. We should note, however, that these results are merely indicative of the short-run effects of the European Economic Community, and say little about the long-term repercussions.

Turning to the second problem of the size of the gains from the union we have several pieces of fragmentary evidence.

P. J. Verdoorn[6] has estimated the expected effects of the formation of a European customs union encompassing not only the countries of the present European Economic Community, but also the Scandinavian countries and the United Kingdom. Depending on the precise assumption made as far as possible exchange rate adjustment is concerned, he estimates that intra-European trade is likely to increase 15 to 19 per cent. Total gains from trade creation are estimated to be $68.8 million, while losses from trade diversion are expected to be $68.0 million, leaving a net gain of less than $1 million as a result of the formation of the union.

A second estimate of the possible welfare effects of freer trade between Britain and the rest of Europe has been made by Harry Johnson.[7] Using trade projections made by the *Economist*'s Intelligence Unit, he concludes that the gains to Britain alone are probably in the neighborhood of £225 million in 1970, roughly 1 per cent of the expected Gross National Product.

[5] B. Balassa, "Trade Creation and Trade Diversion in the European Common Market," *Economic Journal*, March 1967.

[6] P. J. Verdoorn, "Two Notes on Tariff Reductions," in International Labour Office, *Social Aspects of European Economic Cooperation*, Geneva, 1956.

[7] H. G. Johnson, "The Gains from Freer Trade with Europe: An Estimate," *Manchester School*, September 1958.

Finally, J. Wemelsfelder[8] estimated the effects of lowering Germany's import duties during 1956 and 1957 by more than 50 per cent. The additions to national income due to the lowering of the tariff were estimated to be in the neighborhood of 375 million German marks, roughly one-fifth of one per cent of total national income. While these results have no direct bearing on the customs union issue, they nevertheless suggest the order of magnitude of the effects due to tariff elimination.

Even if we allow an error of 100 per cent in all the estimates cited, we still find that none of the numerical data available suggests sizable gains due to the formation of customs unions. But we should point out again that these estimates of gains refer to static gains only. Dynamic gains may be expected to be higher, but in the absence of at least fragmentary empirical evidence, it is difficult to say anything concrete.

SUGGESTED FURTHER READINGS

Balassa, Bela, *The Theory of Economic Integration.* Homewood, Ill.: Richard D. Irwin, 1961.

———, "Trade Creation and Trade Diversion in the European Common Market," *Economic Journal,* March 1967.

Corden, Max, "Recent Developments in the Theory of International Trade," *Special Papers in International Economics,* No. 7, International Finance Section, Princeton University, 1965, Chapter 5.

Johnson, Harry, "The Gains from Freer Trade with Europe," *Manchester School,* September 1958.

———, *Money, Trade, and Economic Growth.* Cambridge: Harvard University Press, 1962, Chapter 3.

Lipsey, R., and K. Lancaster, "The General Theory of Second Best," *Review of Economic Studies,* October 1956.

Lipsey, Richard, "The Theory of Customs Unions," *Economic Journal,* September 1960.

Meade, James, *The Theory of Customs Unions.* Amsterdam: North Holland Publications, 1955.

Scitovsky, Tibor, *Economic Theory and Western European Integration.* London: Allen & Unwin, 1962, Chapters 1, 3.

Vanek, Jaroslav, *International Trade: Theory and Economic Policy.* Homewood, Ill.: Richard D. Irwin, 1962, Chapter 18.

Viner, Jacob, *The Customs Union Issue.* New York: Carnegie Endowment for International Peace, 1950.

[8] J. Wemelsfelder, "The Short-Term Effect of the Lowering of Import Duties in Germany," *Economic Journal,* March 1960.

The Closed Economy: A Review of Some Basic Concepts

A self-sufficient country produces all the goods that its inhabitants consume. The analysis of a self-sufficient country, often referred to as a *closed economy*, will serve as a review of some of the basic economic concepts to be employed in our analysis of an *open economy*, i.e., a country which engages in international trade. Naturally, it is impossible to give a complete review of the relevant economic theory in this appendix, and the reader is referred to any of the many excellent textbooks available on the subject.

1. Production

a. The Production Possibility Curve

The total volume of productive resources available to any country is generally fixed at any given point in time. There is only so much land available, the population and therefore the size of the labor force are given, and the quantity of man-made resources (capital equipment) is fixed.[1]

The productive resources, or factors of production, can be used to produce commodities desired by the inhabitants of the country. Because the amount of factors of production is limited, we will be able to produce only

[1] This assumption holds true, of course, only within limits. If prices paid for land went up, more "marginal" land might be pressed into use: deserts might be irrigated, swamps be drained, lakes or ocean bays be filled in. Similarly, if wages were to increase, the size of the labor force would increase because people would be willing to perform overtime work for the higher wages, housewives might take on a job, people would postpone retirement, or the like. Yet, as a first approximation, it might be useful to assume that the quantities of factors of production available are fixed.

172

a limited amount of commodities. As long as their desires are not completely satiated, consumers will want to have more of the commodities than can be produced with the available resources. This makes it necessary to choose between different products the country can produce with its limited factors of production.

To simplify matters we will assume that there are only two commodities that our country (or, if you prefer, our Robinson Crusoe on his island) produces: cloth and wheat. If we devote all our resources to the production of cloth, there will be a maximum amount of cloth which we can produce, *given* the technologically most efficient way to produce cloth and, of course, our fixed amount of resources. Also, there will be a maximum amount of wheat which can be produced if we devote all our resources to wheat production.

Naturally, it is also possible to produce various combinations of cloth and wheat. For each additional unit of wheat that we want to produce, we must reduce cloth production to free the additional resources needed for wheat production.

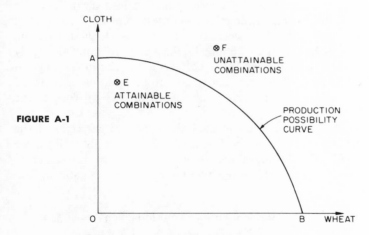

FIGURE A-1

The maximum wheat/cloth combinations which can be produced delineate our production possibilities. These possibilities can be depicted graphically. In Figure A-1 we show the quantity of wheat along the horizontal axis and the quantity of cloth along the vertical axis. The maximum cloth/wheat combinations which can be produced are then plotted on the graph. The collection of all these points depicts the *production possibility curve* AB for the country.

b. Technological Efficiency

All the points on the production possibility curve are *efficient* in a technological sense: given our resources and production techniques, it is not possible to produce more of one commodity without reducing the output of the other commodity. From this definition of technological efficiency it follows that all points that lie below and to the left of the production possibility curve AB are technologically inefficient points of production.

Product combinations which can be attained with our resources and production techniques are often referred to as the *attainable set* or the *attainable combination of commodities*. The attainable set includes all technologically efficient (the points on the curve) as well as all technologically inefficient (the points below the curve) product combinations. Naturally, we are most interested in the maximum attainable product combinations which are represented by the borderline of the attainable set, i.e., the production possibility curve.

There are two major reasons for the nonattainment of a technologically efficient output combination. First, some of our resources may be unemployed or underemployed: factories may be working below capacity, workers may be out of work, and natural resources may lie idle. But it is also possible that even with all resources fully employed we are still not producing at a point located on the production possibility curve. This will be true if there are inefficiencies in how we use our productive resources: some of the factors of production are not used in the place where their return is the highest, resulting in output which falls below its maximum level. We might think of highly trained engineers driving trucks, while truckdrivers are trying to design complex technical equipment. Obviously, aggregate output could be increased if the truckdrivers were to drive the trucks and leave the design work to the engineers.

Output combinations which are located above and to the right of the production possibility curve are termed *unattainable* or infeasible. Given the amount of resources available and the state of the technology, it will not be possible to produce output combinations that fall in this unattainable region.

c. Opportunity Costs and the Marginal Rate of Transformation

We have already stated that it is possible to expand the production of one commodity, provided we are willing to cut down on the production of the other commodity. The amount of wheat that must be sacrificed to obtain an additional unit of cloth is often referred to in the literature as the *opportunity cost* of producing this second commodity. The term opportunity cost calls our attention to the fact that in order to produce one commodity we have to forego the opportunity of producing other commodities. The opportunity cost of production may vary (see below) as we move along the production possibility curve.

The rate at which we have to sacrifice one commodity in order to obtain one additional unit of the other commodity is also referred to as the *marginal rate of transformation* in production (MRT). Graphically, the MRT is shown

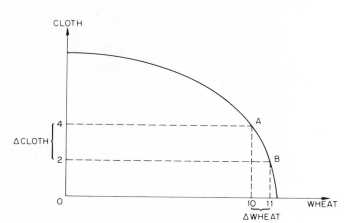

FIGURE A-2

by the (negative) slope of the production possibility curve. Consider Figure A-2. At point A the country is producing 4 units of cloth and 10 units of wheat. In order to expand the production of wheat by one unit the country will have to sacrifice two units of cloth. In other words: the opportunity cost of the eleventh wheat unit is 2 cloth units; or, to use our present terminology, the rate at which cloth production can be transformed into wheat production is two to one at the margin, i.e., the MRT is equal to 2. This, however, is also the (negative) slope of the production possibility curve between the points A and B.[2]

We can write:

$$\text{MRT}_{\text{WC}} = -\frac{\Delta \text{ Cloth}}{\Delta \text{ Wheat}} \qquad \text{(A-1)}$$

d. Increasing, Decreasing, and Constant Opportunity Costs

The various factors influencing the shape of the production possibility curve are discussed in greater detail in Chapter 3. Here, however, we have to pay attention briefly to the implications that arise out of the different possible shapes of the production possibility curves. Viewed from the origin, the production possibility curve may appear as concave (Figure A-3), convex (Figure A-4), or as a straight line (Figure A-5).

If the production possibility curve is concave as viewed from the origin, it indicates the existence of increasing opportunity costs for the two commodities. As the output of one commodity is expanded, we will have to give up

---

[2] Actually, the slope of the production possibility curve changes slightly between points A and B. What we are measuring here is the slope of a straight line through A and B. Yet, as we make the distance between A and B smaller and smaller and finally infinitesimally small, this line will finally become the tangent to the production possibility curve.

successively larger quantities of the other commodity in order to obtain equal increases in the output of the first commodity. Successive units of wheat become more and more expensive in terms of cloth, indicating that the opportunity cost of obtaining additional units of cloth increases. It is also possible to show the process in reverse: if we want to obtain more and more units of cloth, we have to sacrifice ever larger amounts of wheat.

The case of decreasing opportunity costs is shown in Figure A-4. Here the production of additional units of wheat requires the sacrifice of successively smaller amounts of cloth.

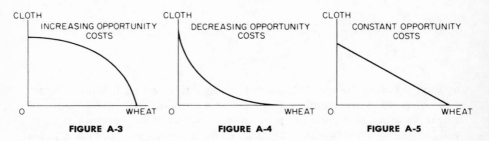

FIGURE A-3   FIGURE A-4   FIGURE A-5

The case of constant opportunity costs is illustrated in Figure A-5. For each additional unit of wheat we will always have to give up equal amounts of cloth. The opportunity cost of wheat production in terms of cloth is the same throughout the range of production possibilities, resulting in a straight line production possibility curve.

e. Two Factors of Production

(i) Isoquants

The basic geometric tool used to analyze the two-factor case is the *isoquant*, also referred to as an *equal product contour*. An isoquant is defined as the locus of all efficient input or factor of production combinations which will yield the same quantity of output. The quantities of the two inputs which are employed in the production of the output are measured along the two axes. In Figure A-6 inputs of labor (L) are measured along the horizontal axis, while inputs of capital (K) are measured along the vertical axis.

From the technological information given to us, we are able to derive a whole map of isoquants for different levels of output. The isoquant map will fill the input space shown in Figure A-6.

The slope of an isoquant is often referred to as the *marginal rate of factor substitution* (MRFS). The marginal rate of factor substitution gives the quantity by which one factor has to be increased if the other factor is decreased, while the total quantity of output stays constant. The loss in output from the reduction of one factor must be made up by the increase in output resulting

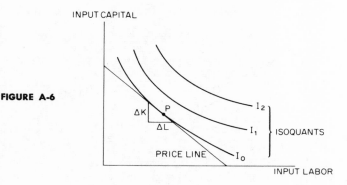

FIGURE A-6

from the increase of the other factor. The slope of the isoquant shows the quantity of K which must be added (or subtracted) divided by the quantity of L which must be subtracted (or added) in order to maintain a constant level of output. The negative slope ($-\Delta K/\Delta L$) is defined as the marginal rate of factor substitution.

$$\text{MRFS}_{LK} = -\frac{\Delta K}{\Delta L} \tag{A-2}$$

If we are interested in finding out which is actually the most efficient combination of inputs to be used in the production of a given quantity of output, we have to introduce *relative factor prices* into our analysis. The slope of the price line for the two factors of production ($-\Delta K/\Delta L$ in Figure A-6) shows the relative factor prices. The optimal combination of inputs is found at the point where the price line is tangent to the isoquant representing the desired output level. Such a point is given by P in Figure A-6. At point P the following conditions are fulfilled:

$$\text{MRFS}_{LK} = -\frac{\Delta K}{\Delta L} \equiv \frac{P_L}{P_K} \tag{A-3}$$

The marginal rate of factor substitution is equal to the relative price ratio.

There are four characteristics of isoquants that are worth bearing in mind: (1) Isoquants slope downward to the right. If the output level is to remain constant, a decrease of one input will have to be compensated for by an increase of another input. (2) Isoquants are convex to the origin. This is because, in general, successive reductions by equally large amounts of one

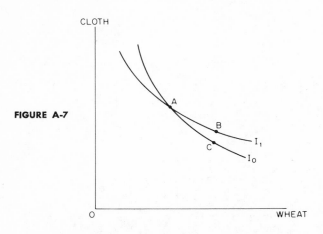

FIGURE A-7

factor will have to be compensated for by larger and larger additions of the substitute factor. Another way of expressing the same idea is to say that the rate at which two factors of production can be substituted for each other diminishes. (3) Isoquants cannot intersect. This is easily shown with the help of Figure A-7. Input combinations A and C are on the same isoquant I_0, yielding an equal quantity of output. The same is true about A and B, both of which are located on isoquant I_1. But if A yields the same output as B, and it is also true that A yields the same output as C, then B and C must yield the same output, too. As all input combinations yielding the same quantity of output constitute an isoquant, B and C should also be located on the same isoquant—which they are not, according to Figure A-7. Also, input combination B contains more of both inputs and should therefore yield a higher output than C. Clearly, we have a contradiction which can be eliminated only by postulating that isoquants cannot intersect. (4) Isoquants that are located farther away from the origin denote higher levels of output than isoquants closer to the origin. There will be an isoquant through every point of our input space.

In general we are interested not only in the determination of one specific efficient factor combination, but also in the locus of the efficient factor combinations for each level of output. In other words, we want to derive the point of tangency of the factor price ratio with *all* isoquants. The locus of all these tangency positions is called an *expansion path* and shows the efficient factor combinations for all output levels, given the relative factor price ratio. An expansion path is shown in Figure A-8.

(ii) Homogeneous Isoquants

Among all possible sets of isoquants, there is one particular set which has attracted much attention from economists, homogeneous isoquants. A homogeneous set of isoquants is defined as a map of isoquants characterized

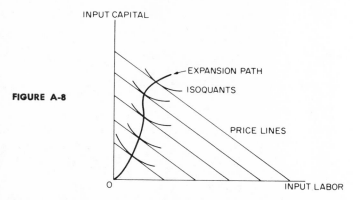

FIGURE A-8

by the fact that each isoquant has an identical slope at its intersection with any straight line through the origin. (See Figure A-9.) Viewed from the origin, each isoquant represents, therefore, an exact blown-up image of lower isoquants.

If there are linear, i.e., constant, returns to scale, then we have a set of *linear homogeneous isoquants.* In such a set of isoquants, a doubling of *all* inputs leads to a doubling of the level of output—i.e., the additions to output produced by a given addition to all inputs are the same, no matter what the level of output—and we have constant or linear returns to scale. Any isoquant showing twice the amount of output as another isoquant will be exactly twice as far removed from the origin as the other isoquant.

(iii) *Factor Intensity*

Often, we are interested in the production of not only one commodity, but of two (or more) commodities. In Figure A-10 we show the sets of iso-

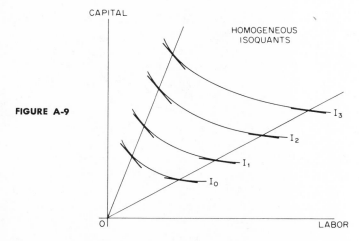

FIGURE A-9

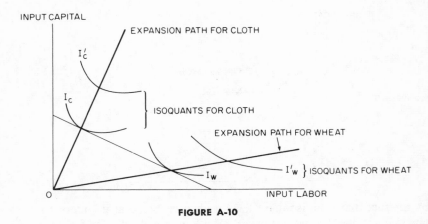

FIGURE A-10

quants of two commodities, cloth and wheat. It is now possible to say something about the *relative intensity* with which the two factors are used in the production of the two commodities. Thus, for any given relative price ratio, cloth production uses relatively (to wheat production) more capital and less labor at all output levels. On the other hand, wheat production uses relatively (to cloth production) more labor than capital. One can, then, refer to cloth production as being relatively capital intensive, and to wheat production as being relatively labor intensive. Note that the absolute amounts of the two factors used in production do not have to be specified. It is not *absolute* factor intensities that count here, but merely *relative* factor intensities. This enables us to avoid the thorny problem of having to decide on the appropriate unit of measurement for the two dissimilar factors of production.

(iv) *The Edgeworth Box Diagram*

In order to show the efficient combinations of inputs to be used in the production of the two outputs we utilize an *Edgeworth Box diagram*. In Figure A-11 we show the set of isoquants for wheat production drawn in its usual position, while the set of isoquants for cloth production is drawn upside down and with sides reversed. Thus the origin of the coordinate system for cloth production lies in the upper righthand corner of the box. The size of the box shows the total factor endowments (factor supplies) available to the country. The vertical size shows the total quantity of capital available, while the horizontal size shows the total quantity of labor available.

We are now interested in establishing which input combinations will be efficient in the sense that no reallocation of inputs would lead to an increase in the level of output of one commodity *without* decreasing the level of output for the other commodity. All points of tangency of two isoquants represent such *technologically efficient input combinations*.

The line connecting all technologically efficient input combinations such

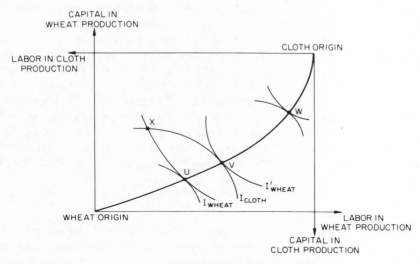

FIGURE A-11

as U, V, and W in Figure A-11 is called the *contract curve*. At the points of tangency it will be true that the marginal rate of factor substitution is the same for both commodities. In equation form:

$$(MRFS_{LK})_C = (MRFS_{LK})_W \qquad (A-4)$$

If this condition is not fulfilled, it will always be possible to reallocate some factors of production in such a way that the output of one commodity will be increased (a higher isoquant can be reached), while the output of the other commodity will stay constant. Such a situation is shown by point X, which is not located on the contract curve. Moving from point X to point V does not change the output level of cloth production since we stay on the same isoquant. However, the output of wheat will increase from the output level associated with the isoquant through X (and U) to the higher output level indicated by the isoquant through point V. Thus we are able to increase the total output by reallocating our resources in the fashion indicated. Once a point on the contract curve itself is attained, no reshuffling of resources will help to achieve a higher output level of one commodity without reducing the output level of the other commodity simultaneously: a technologically efficient production pattern has been achieved.

2. Consumption

Production takes place not for its own sake, but only in order to satisfy some further objective: consumption of the goods and services produced. The act of consumption yields utility to the consumer, and the consumer is assumed to maximize the utility obtained from his total consumption. To achieve this goal he should act in a rational manner, which implies—among other things—that his choices should be *transitive*. Transitivity of choices refers to the notion that a consumer who prefers X to Y and also prefers Y to Z will, when confronted with a choice between X and Z, always choose X. A consumer who acts in such a rational way should be able to rank all commodities or commodity bundles in order of preference. In this ordering or ranking the consumer is not assumed to be able to say by how much he prefers one commodity to another commodity; a mere ranking of different commodities will suffice. There also exists the possibility that a consumer is indifferent between two commodity bundles if they yield the same level of utility.

a. Indifference Curves

The possibility that a given level of utility can be derived from many different commodity combinations will occupy our attention somewhat more. If consumption of one commodity is reduced, it will in general be possible to compensate the consumer for this loss in utility by increasing his consumption of another commodity. If the decrease in utility experienced due to the reduced consumption of one commodity is merely offset as the increase in utility due to the increased consumption of another commodity, we may expect that the consumer is indifferent between these two situations because his aggregate or total utility level has remained unchanged.

When we plot all points showing different commodity combinations

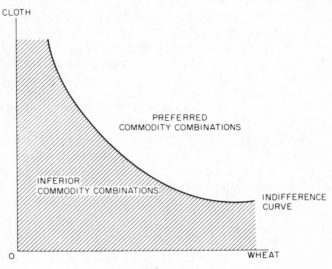

FIGURE A-12

yielding the same level of utility, we are able to derive a so-called *indifference curve* or equal utility contour. The term indifference curve stems from the contention that a consumer should be indifferent between all commodity combinations yielding the same amount of utility to him. Such an indifference curve is shown in Figure A-12.

Indifference curves have properties very similar to those of isoquants: (1) they slope downward to the right, (2) they are convex to the origin, (3) they cannot intersect, and (4) a higher indifference curve denotes a higher level of utility. Indifference curves are distinguished here from isoquants in that we make no attempt to attach numerical values to the level of utility achieved by the consumer, but restrict ourselves to a *ranking* of all commodity bundles in order of preference without stating by how much one bundle is preferred to the other. This type of "better-or-worse" relationship is referred to as an *ordinal* relation; the term *cardinal* relation is applied to a situation in which we are able to specify quantitatively (as in the case of isoquants) how much better or worse off we are.

b. The Marginal Rate of Substitution

A word has to be said about the slope of the indifference curves. We said above that an indifference curve is the combination of all cloth/wheat collections yielding a constant amount of utility to the consumer. In other words, as we move along one indifference curve, the consumer gives up some units of wheat in order to obtain some units of cloth (or vice versa). The rate at which these two commodities can be substituted for each other without changing the level of utility is often called the *marginal rate of substitution* (MRS). Graphically, the slope of the indifference curve is given by the change in the quantity of cloth divided by the change in the quantity of wheat, and the negative of this slope ($-\Delta C/\Delta W$) is defined as the marginal rate of substitution of wheat for cloth. We can write:

$$\text{MRS}_{\text{WC}} = -\frac{\Delta C}{\Delta W} \tag{A-5}$$

3. Maximization

a. Equilibrium

We are now in a position to combine our tools of analysis to derive the country's optimal production and consumption pattern. Let us start with a given production possibility curve reflecting the country's production opportunities and a set of indifference curves depicting the taste patterns of the residents of the country. (See Figure A-13.) Initially, the country in question produces a combination of cloth and wheat shown by point P on the pro-

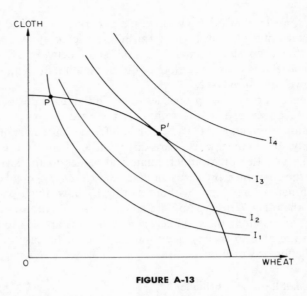

FIGURE A-13

duction possibility curve. If the country does not engage in international trade, point P will also show the amounts of cloth and wheat which are available for consumption. This bundle of goods will allow the residents of the country to achieve the utility level indicated by the indifference curve through P, namely, I_1. If we change the production pattern in such a way that more wheat and less cloth is produced, the residents of the country will be able to reach successively higher indifference curves. At point P' the highest attainable indifference curve is reached, showing that the residents have achieved the highest possible utility level consistent with the country's production possibilities. At point P' the slope of the production possibility curve is equal to the slope of the indifference curve as the two curves are tangent to each other. We will recall that the slope of the production possibility curve shows the marginal rate of transformation, while the slope of the indifference curve shows the marginal rate of substitution.

The point on the production possibility curve at which the indifference curve is tangent is also referred to as an *economically efficient* point. We recall that technological efficiency refers to *all* the points on the production possibility curve. Among the maximum output combinations which can be produced, given our technology and resources, there will be *one* point describing the commodity combination which is economically most desirable in that it allows the country to attain the highest utility level.

b. The Terms of Trade

If production and consumption takes place at point P' (Figure A-14), the two commodities will exchange for each other in the proportion $\Delta C / \Delta W$.

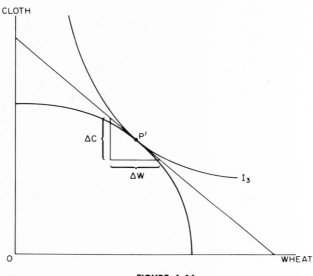

FIGURE A-14

This *physical exchange* ratio is often referred to as the *terms of trade*. Once we know what quantities of the two goods exchange for each other, it is only a small step to the determination of the relative prices of the two commodities. It is clear that the relative prices of the two commodities are inversely related to the quantities of the two goods which can be exchanged for each other. If the price of one of the two commodities rises relatively to the other one, this means that we obtain a smaller quantity of the commodity in exchange for the other commodity than previously.

The terms of trade at which the two commodities will be traded in the market is given by the slope of the tangent to both the production possibility curve and the indifference curve. Point P' in Figure A-14 shows the overall equilibrium condition for a closed economy. At point P' the marginal rates of substitution and transformation are equal to each other and they are equal to the price ratio and the negative inverse of the quantities of the two commodities which exchange for each other.

$$MRS_{WC} = \frac{P_W}{P_C} = -\frac{\Delta C}{\Delta W} = MRT_{WC} \qquad (A-6)$$

Thus the quantities of both commodities produced and consumed, their relative prices, and their physical exchange ratio (terms of trade) are determined.

For a country which does not engage in international trade, the optimal consumption and production pattern is reached when the marginal rate of transformation between any two commodities is equal to the marginal rate of substitution between the same two commodities.

INDEX